Robin Gill is Michael Ramsey Professor of Modern Theology at the University of Kent and an Honorary Canon of Canterbury Cathedral. In his spare time he leads a clergy team serving five rural churches near Maidstone and is also the local Area Dean. He is married to a doctor. Apart from his many academic writings, he wrote the Archbishop of Canterbury's Lent Book for 1992 entitled *Gifts of Love*.

A Sense of Grace

Robin Gill

First published in Great Britain in 2004 by
Society for Promoting Christian Knowledge
Holy Trinity Church
Marylebone Road
London NW1 4DU

British Library Cataloguing-in-Publication Data

A catalogue record for this book is available from the British Library

ISBN 0–281–05630–7

1 3 5 7 9 10 8 6 4 2

Typeset by Avocet Typeset, Chilton, Aylesbury, Bucks
Printed in Great Britain by Bookmarque Ltd, Croydon, Surrey

Contents

Contents

Preface

This book is written for busy people. A short meditation for every day, except Sunday, during the six weeks of Lent. Perhaps you will read it last thing at night before going to sleep. Or perhaps first thing in the morning (wearing glasses in bed is such a pain for those of us who need them).

Grace is a rich theme. It makes vital connections between everyday life and Christian faith, between the secular and the sacred. It helps us to understand our need of God. And it can deepen our understanding of Jesus as Son of God.

I do hope that you enjoy reading *A of Sense of Grace*. I have loved writing it.

All the Bible passages come from the *New Revised Standard Version*.

WEEK 1

Graceful Living

———·•·———

1

In love with Grace

A joke was played on my grandfather when he was a young curate. Horace (that really was his name) Hammond was ordained in 1909 and was a curate for the next 12 years, first in the diocese of Bath and Wells and then in Canterbury. Eventually, after this long apprenticeship, he became vicar of Elmsted and Hastingleigh, near Canterbury, in 1921.

I can remember him shortly before retirement as rector of Ruckinge, just on the edge of Romney Marsh, in the 1950s. As a young boy I was always intrigued by him and could think of nothing better than being a country vicar just like him. He shaved with a cut-throat razor in the morning and went to the Ashford cattle market every week. Riddled with arthritis, a photograph shows him beaming broadly while clutching the two walking sticks that supported him. Because walking was so slow and painful he exercised his fierce mongrel dog, Topsy, by driving in front of him along the country lanes in an old Austin. He always smiled in church, recycled sermons from one year to the next and loved visiting parishioners. They in turn loved him and, when my grandmother died, they loved him even more.

I last saw him in 1967, just days before getting married myself. By then he was 82 and in hospital, he was now tired and eager to see his own wife and parents again. Those around him talked about living longer and getting better. They enthused about all the things that he would be doing when he got out of hospital. But he looked knowingly at me instead. And then he died peacefully the day after our wedding and just ten months before I was ordained. We never quite made it into *Crockford's Clerical Directory* together.

Early in his first curacy he fell in love with Grace, a journalist's daughter, and eventually married her in January 1912. Then sadly in April his own father, himself a country vicar (I know, it runs in the family) collapsed and died.

Those were the days of plentiful curates, all of them young men (not women) of course. Naturally they teased each other continuously. One of his fellow curates noticed that Horace always left the notes for his sermon in the pulpit just before the service started – probably the same notes that he was still using nearly five decades later. On this particular Sunday the text was 2 Corinthians 12.9: 'My grace is sufficient for you', or, in the words of the King James Bible, 'My grace is sufficient for thee'.

When my grandfather climbed into the pulpit and looked down at his notes he began to flush and giggle. A carefully prepared sermon was completely wrecked and, doubtless, the vicar in charge was as furious as members of the congregation were delighted. The problem was that his fellow curate had changed the word 'thee' to 'me', and perhaps also drawn attention to the words that follow [again quoting the King James Bible]: 'for my power is made perfect in weakness. Most gladly therefore will I rather glory in my weaknesses.'

We will return to this great biblical text later in the fifth week. It is one of the most extraordinary accounts of the Christian life. Paul writes intimately about a profound mystical experience, then about some 'thorn in the flesh', and finally about an overwhelming sense of grace. It has given Christians ever since a unique insight into the single most important feature of the Christian way of life. Indeed, if I had to choose a phrase to capture what is really distinctive about this way of life, it is just this . . . *a sense of grace*. However, Paul is for later in this book. Most of the biblical meditations this week will be drawn, instead, from Mark, the earliest of the four Gospels.

The story about my grandfather is a useful reminder that 'grace' in the English language has many different meanings. It can be a woman's name, a measure of beauty, a goddess, a respite, a small musical note, a gratuitous embellishment, a prayer and many other things besides. There is much exploring to be done before we can arrive at a fuller Christian understanding of grace. At its most basic, 'grace' for Christians usually involves a sense that God is helping us in our lives. For the moment that can serve as a minimum understanding of grace.

The aim of this book is to expand upon this minimum understanding, to explore a variety of ideas about grace and, finally, to reach a fuller understanding of a sense of grace.

This week I will make this exploration using family photographs. Of course these are my family's photographs. But I will leave you to imagine them, since I would rather that you let your own family photographs tell a similar story.

MEDITATION
Mark 1.16–20

2

Innocent grace

The photograph of my grandfather that I treasure most was taken shortly before his ordination. It shows him looking slightly embarrassed and awkward at a family tea party on the vicarage lawn at Westoning in Bedfordshire.

He stands with his cousin Reggie behind his parents who are seated at a gate-legged tea table in the foreground. My great-grandfather (the vicar) has a high Edwardian dog collar and silver hair and beard. He struggles hard to smile to camera as he holds a teacup precariously in his hand and tries to sit forward on a collapsible deckchair. My great-grandmother, looking benevolent but formidable on a higher dining-room chair, gazes to the right of the camera. Wearing a full-length Edwardian dress with lace, ribbons and frills, she is poised just about to pour from a silver teapot. Reggie, himself wearing a fashionable Edwardian suit, together with a gold watch chain across his waistcoat, smiles in a relaxed manner. Horace doesn't smile at all, but stands in a sports jacket with his left hand in his trouser pocket and his right hand holding a plate of sandwiches. Like many a son his expression seems to say, 'Do we really have to do this?'

Doubtless the photographer had been intrusive on that sunny afternoon. Everything in the photograph has been carefully staged. The growing shadows across the lawn, the fir trees set in the middle of the background, the flowerbeds carefully groomed, the lace tablecloth straightened, and the table balanced (just). A fairly long time-exposure would have been needed for the photograph. Only Reggie escaped holding something in his hand until it ached and he alone affects an apparently genuine smile. The others are all actors – husband,

4

wife and son – frozen in a graceful vicarage family tea party.

What next? Did my great-grandmother spill the tea? After all she is not actually looking at the teapot. Did my great-grandfather's deckchair collapse? It is set at the highest notch and even then only just allows him to reach the table. Did my grandfather become the stroppy son and walk away? In later life he started to hum when he heard a family row erupting. Did Reggie remain polite? As he grew older it was realized that he was an alcoholic. Who knows?

With help as ever from hindsight, this photograph seems to capture a moment of innocent grace. As you already know, my great-grandfather was soon to die (he was only 62 but looks older in the photograph) and my great-grandmother would, as a result, have to leave her beloved vicarage. And Reggie died young from his alcoholism.

Soon this graceful Edwardian age was to collapse. Dying in 1912 my great-grandfather knew nothing about the calamity of the Great War or the Depression that followed it. Most of his life had been spent with the old Queen Victoria as monarch, but now there was the new and popular reign of the rakish King Edward VII. Life was comfortable for the middle classes and most remained confident that it would stay so. How wrong they were.

The innocent grace apparently captured in the photograph has clearly been staged. Shoes are highly polished and laundry is beautifully white. The silver shines brightly and hair has been carefully brushed. Yet tragedy, both personal and national, is horribly near. The image is crafted to convey graceful living and a family that is content with its place in the world. Perhaps that is how it really felt at the time. Or perhaps tensions were already present. What if Reggie had in reality been drinking before the photograph was taken and the rest of the disapproving family were pretending not to notice? What if my great-grandfather's health was already failing and the others were trying hard not to show how anxious they were about this? What if the family had been squabbling about posing for the photograph and were now attempting to look relaxed? What if ...

One of the features of graceful living is that it is transient. The awkward edges of life soon upset it. Another of its features is that it tends to be concerned more with appearance than with reality. This photograph was staged for posterity, to give yet-to-be-born relatives a good image of their forebears long after their death. And that is what it does. Yet it still contains hints of contrivance almost a century after my relatives staged that classic vicarage tea party. Innocent grace portrayed, even manufactured.

Yet such 'innocent grace' was soon lost as Europe descended into the appalling world wars that were to scar the rest of the century.

MEDITATION
Mark 7.1–8

3

Grace in a garden

Eventually my great-grandmother came to live with Horace (by now vicar of Brenzett, Snargate and Snave on Romney Marsh) and Grace. A photograph taken in the 1930s shows her sitting 'gracefully' in the vicarage garden.

Unlike the photograph taken a quarter-of-a-century earlier, this one is no longer staged for posterity. It is simply a snap taken on a box camera of an old lady enjoying the sunshine next to a fruit tree pinned to the tall garden wall. She is still wearing a long Edwardian dress, but this time it lacks frills and bows. This is no longer a matriarch controlling all around her, but an elderly grandmother smiling serenely to camera. A graceful moment captured near the end of her life.

But perhaps not quite so graceful for Grace herself. Mother-in-law's presence in the house may not have been particularly welcome. For whatever reason, she went on holiday just up the coast to Walmer with her daughter Mary Grace (my mother), but without Horace or mother-in-law.

Whatever the relationship between mother-in-law and daughter-in-law, the relationship between Mary Grace and her grandmother was clearly affectionate. For the rest of her life my mother kept a small postcard from her grandmother written while they were on holiday at Walmer:

Sunday 3 August, 1934
Dear Mary,
Thank you for P.C. I am so glad to hear that we shall not be able to recognize you and Mummy when you return home this week, the sea air must have done wonders for you both. Daddy has had a Wedding at Brenzett, and there is another

one this month. We went to tea again at Snargate. We still get very bad bites. Mrs H has a bad knee.

Love from the animals and myself.
Grandma

The little preoccupations of an affectionate postcard across the generations; a shared love of animals; yet another tea party; the wedding; bites from Marsh mosquitoes; and, inevitably, a mention of elderly infirmities. She was remembered in the family for enjoying food, especially fresh plums. Whenever it was the season for them she was teased for giving herself indigestion . . . that is until she died later that year from stomach cancer. Grace soon gave way to a sense of family guilt.

A sense of grace in the beauty and pleasures of a country garden or of a holiday by the sea are real even if fleeting. They live long in our imaginations and feed our sense of nostalgia. Memories of childhood in the summer when the sun always shone and gardens flowered unattended. Sandy beaches and blue seas without crowds of other people. Or virginal snow without human footprints in any direction. Meadows with white lambs playing together among the cowslips. There is a real sense of grace to be found in these 'memories'. Fleeting, elusive and often imagined, but grace nonetheless.

I think that is why we tend to fill our family photograph albums with such images. It not only allows us to remember, it also makes it possible for us to imagine . . . imagine a world without difficulties and problems, a world when the sun always shines, a world in which people smile and are always nice to each other. And when we discover pictures of ourselves that hint of some less perfect world, we are strongly tempted to tear them out from the family album altogether.

In many family albums there are indeed suspicious gaps. It is not simply personal vanity that causes these gaps (although, of course, it may be a factor). It is also evidence of an attempt to reconstruct the past. Dictators notoriously do this – constructing images of their past that have little relation to reality. Stalin, Mao and Saddam Hussein all did as much. But, to a lesser degree, we would all like to do that. 'Remembering' some uninterrupted graceful past is all too natural.

Yet there is more to it even than that. Moments of heightened experience, even fleeting moments, can act as powerful markers in our imaginations. Many religious people will be well aware of this – but that is for later. For the moment, there is something very important to most people about recalling moments of heightened experience even years later. A sense of grace – evoked by a beautiful house or garden or by some great natural beauty or even just by blissful weather – lives on in our imaginations and adds real value to our daily lives.

Who each one of us is as a person is at least partially shaped by these moments of grace.

MEDITATION
Mark 9.2–8

4

Grace in animals

And there is a sense of grace to be found in our response to animals. All of my mother's family were in love with dogs, a love that is still passing down the generations.

There is another pair of photographs, this time from the 1940s, of my grandfather in front of the rectory at Ruckinge holding Topsy. He is being licked on the chin by this ill-tempered dog, yet is again smiling broadly to the camera. It stirs one of my earliest memories; the sound, sight and almost feel of Topsy's wet tongue scraping on my grandfather's stubble.

Grace and Horace were delighted to be offered the living at Ruckinge in 1935. It had a new and smaller rectory, more suitable for a meagre clerical income than the rambling vicarage at Brenzett. And they no longer had mother-in-law to care for and perhaps to squabble over. The rectory overlooked the beautiful church at Ruckinge, with its tower shaped like an owl's head. Reputedly Grace had to humour the Bishop of Dover before Horace was offered the living, and even then it was one of the poorest livings around. Left to his own devices he lacked any form of clerical ambition and had no aspiration to being anything other than a country vicar.

But 1935 was not a good year to become a Church of England vicar. English farmers were in the middle of a sustained (and soon successful) battle against tithes. A fading photograph from *The News Chronicle* for 18 October shows a police guard outside Ruckinge church as parishioners arrived for the induction service for my grandfather. In the weeks that followed he was to visit several of the local farmers in prison. He was deeply embarrassed that his income still depended upon enforced tithes, raised from farmers whether they were Anglicans or not. He soon won and then retained their strong friendship.

By the 1940s the tithes had been abolished and Horace, Grace and Topsy could enjoy their rectory together. Grace sent her own mother a card saying:

Dear mother
This is a photo of the road in front of our dear little Church and House
                    Grace

One of the photographs they took themselves shows the rectory from just inside the church porch. Another shows the rectory taken from the garden, with an ancient, and now protected, oak, with a wood-store in its hollow trunk, in the foreground. And the other two show my grandfather before and after being licked.

Why are some families so in love with dogs? Doubtless some would see dogs as child substitutes. After all, we take puppies from their mothers when they are only two or three months old. They then bond to us as if we are the pack leaders. We train them to live in our houses, probably swap numerous germs with them and habitually treat them as if they were members of the family.

Yet in many families children and dogs are brought up together and can hardly be thought of as substitutes for each other. The relationship between humans and dogs is complicated. It tends to be mutually complementary. Children and dogs play 'tag' quite spontaneously. Old people often believe that dogs are important for protection. Dogs, in turn, get food, water, warmth and shelter without having to search for them. And both dogs and humans appear to like each other's company, smell and touch. For some people, such as my grandfather, this includes being licked on the face by a dog, but for most of us it probably doesn't!

Dogs often appeal to humans for their 'gracefulness', for the way they move their legs, bodies and faces. Those of us who live with dogs learn to interpret their gestures: the look of anticipation when a walk might be imminent; of dejection when it is not; of alertness when a novel sound is heard; of hunger when food is due. Those not brought up with dogs often misinterpret their body language (as most of us do that of wolves) and put themselves in danger as a result. In turn, dogs learn to interpret our body language and anticipate our movements from our ritual actions. They soon learn the word 'walk' (as children we had to avoid the word altogether in the presence of our pet mongrel), or they notice when we go for our coat or their leads.

There is a sense of grace at the heart of this intricate and long relationship between dogs and humans. Something is given beyond ourselves. In truth, for those of us who are dog-lovers, life without a dog always has something missing.

MEDITATION
Mark 11.1–10

5

Stoical grace

Grace inherited some money when her own parents died. It meant that she was no longer dependent upon Horace's stipend of £400 a year. So she used it on family holidays to Switzerland.

There is a whole family album for 1936 and 1938 showing a mixture of winter skiing and spring walks at Adelboden high in the Swiss mountains. Grace added humorous captions to many of the photographs. Against a photograph of herself perched on a fence with snowy mountains in the background she writes 'on the rocks'. My grandfather never appears as a skier but only as a walker. Dressed in black brogues, baggy grey trousers, open-necked shirt and battered panama hat, she affectionately refers to him as 'the tramp'. My grandmother, in contrast, walks in a fashionable polka-dot dress together with hiking boots or poses elegantly on long skis, dressed in the thick woollen ski-wear of the day. In some photographs my 20-year-old mother poses alongside her on skis too, but far more reticently (she always hated being photographed).

Sometimes there are new-found friends in these photographs, roped together on a glacier, encountered while walking or gathered around the swimming pool at Adelboden. Other photographs simply show Swiss landscapes, great waterfalls, meadows with spring flowers or snow-clad mountains. After two decades of living as a relatively impoverished priest's wife, she at last had enough money to have family holidays abroad. The theme throughout most of this album of photographs is that of a happy family surrounded by beautiful nature. Grace abounding.

Then there is a gap in the album. It was wartime. Horace

and Grace's early married life had of course been scarred first by the Great War and then by the economic depression of the 1920s. And now it was war again. The 1930s had been just a stay for them in one of the bleakest times of modern history. Their generation uniquely experienced the full force of two world wars with all the hardship it brought to ordinary lives. In the three parishes that they had served, young parishioners were lost in both of these terrible wars.

Ruckinge escaped the London blitz, although it did experience the terror of flying bombs at the very end of the 1939–45 war. And, with their son in the army and their daughter in London, Horace and Grace, like many other parents at the time, had much to worry about. When was it all to end?

By 1949, when the photographs start again, Grace looks ill and tired. She was to die the following spring just short of her sixty-third birthday. She no longer smiles to camera. Despite having grandchildren whom she adored and living in a country now liberated, her kidneys were failing. Looking at the photographs of her sad face today, I cannot be sure whether I actually remember her or whether I just remember her through these familiar photographs. I do remember the toys that she placed on our beds whenever we stayed at Ruckinge and I can remember the rows of jars of her homemade jam on the highest shelves in our bedroom. And I can also remember the house and garden becoming ever more neglected (and, of course that was much more fascinating to us as children) in the years following her death. But I am still not sure whether I really do remember her. Nevertheless, her charm, courage and presence shine out from the photographs, and finally her stoicism in the face of death.

In one photograph she sits in her favourite chair at Ruckinge, surrounded by small pieces of family silver on a Victorian trolley. She is propped up with pillows to ease her pain and rests her head on her hand. Her lips are pursed in an attempt to smile, but the smile has gone. She seems to be willing herself to live, while knowing that in reality she is dying.

The term 'grace' is not always used to indicate that someone or something is 'graceful'. It can also signal a pause or moment of respite and sometimes even a reprieve. There was to be no reprieve here, but a sense of pause is captured in what was to be a painful and distressing process of dying. Families often treasure these moments. In Mark's Gospel the flow of the narrative tends to be interrupted by such moments of grace – as when Jesus, sitting in the temple, notices a poor widow donating her two small copper coins (Mark 12.42).

Earlier generations liked to collect the last words of those just about to die. Samuel Pepys was fascinated by the final words of those on the scaffold. He witnessed a number of executions following the recriminations once monarchy was restored under Charles II. Victorian artists also loved to depict famous death scenes and final farewells.

For Grace her last moments are now lost. She died in hospital and family memories were too painful to be passed down through the generations. Yet this photograph still exists. Despite grieving whenever she saw it, my mother kept it until she died herself half-a-century later. Grace remembered.

———◆———

MEDITATION
Mark 12.41–43

6

Grace across generations

One final family photograph. This time it is of myself at the age of two. More accurately, it is a photograph, taken in 1946, of my twin sister and myself being held by our father. For most of my life I have detested this photograph.

The trouble is that it is every mother's dream and every son's nightmare. I have long, golden curls, I am distinctly over-weight and, disastrously, I appear to be wearing something very like a dress. I am also grinning inanely to myself while my father and sister smile more appropriately to the camera. Looking young and fit and wearing a short-sleeved shirt, my father, already a consultant physician with considerable exper-ience of paediatrics, holds us both proudly.

To capture this moment my parents paid for a professional photographer to come to our garden in north London. Some of the photographs show us sitting on little deckchairs and others playing. Some of them include our older brother, but others not. But it was this photograph that was always one of my mother's favourites. It is really not at all difficult to see why. Yet, just as obviously, it certainly was not mine. Just imagine what my schoolfriends would have said if they had ever been able to see it. It is just the kind of embarrassing pic-ture that relatives love to put in local papers of adults who are trying to celebrate some significant birthday. For years it made me squirm.

And then, very recently and quite unexpectedly, it became my favourite too.

My grandson turned two and produced the same golden curls on a stocky frame – but no dress, thank goodness. A new family photograph of me holding my grandson, in the same manner that my father had held me, was soon set alongside that 1946 photograph. My response was totally changed. A photograph that had been well-hidden in the bottom of a drawer for so many years is now proudly displayed in our house. And I can even tolerate the continuing family jokes about the dress . . .

As other grandparents will know, having grandchildren brings such unexpected pleasures. We did enjoy being parents immensely, but being a parent carries so many responsibilities while being a grandparent carries so few. The panic that young parents know when they first have a tiny baby in the house. This little life is totally dependent upon you. You must feed and care for this baby and then bring him or her up as responsibly as you can. Just days before you had the freedom to go out when you pleased, but now your life is tied down by this tiny life. Will you be able to make a good parent? Will you be calm and caring? Will you even cope?

Grandparents already know the answer to those questions. We have the huge advantage of having been through it already. And, in any case, as the cliché goes, most of us can hand the grandchildren back. They are not our final responsibility. Yet they are an enormous joy.

At present I can think of few other joys that come near to a day looking after our grandchild. Watching the grandchild crawl (amazing), then walk and begin to talk. Agreeing on what names to be called (often the same names as our own favourite grandparents) and then experiencing the delight at hearing the grandchild address us by those names. Enjoying children's stories, videos and television together. Preparing endless bottles of milk and marmite sandwiches. Going for the first time to a cinema with the grandchild or to the London Aquarium. Looking at stained-glass windows in churches through infant eyes or at the carvings on gravestones outside. Walking slowly through woods hearing every bird sound afresh or examining unexpectedly beautiful weeds. Playing with a hose on a hot day or sledging on a snowy one. Childish joys shared across the generations. We love being grand-parents.

And there is a real sense of grace involved in being a grand-parent. Many of us make links back to our own grandparents as we play with our grandchildren. Somehow five generations become linked in a single moment. Long-dead grandparents live on in our memories and actions. In the voices of our small grandchildren we can hear familiar voices reaching down the generations.

A crucial feature of grace is that we are no longer in full control. Again, something is given beyond ourselves. More than that, we are surprised and delighted by what is given. We see ourselves, not as isolated individuals, but as part of one generation heaped upon another.

We may also take a fresh interest in family trees. This tiny grandchild is given a large chart showing all the different people that have contributed to his or her birth, stretching back as far as we are able to go. Grace across generations.

MEDITATION
Psalm 8

WEEK 2

Airs and Graces

7

Graceful playing

I have a passion for Bach. I do enjoy music from many different ages, ranging from plainsong to jazz. Yet, finally, Bach is my real favourite. Why?

If we could give a rational answer to such a question, I suspect that it would reduce music to something other than music. There is only one way to appreciate music properly, and that is simply to listen to it as music. Music is music. It is even a bit odd writing about music. Of course with Bach there is a complex, intelligent and sometimes even mathematical weaving of notes. Yet that alone would not make his work beautiful music. Perhaps a keyboard player might understand his music better (I am only a very amateur brass player). Yet, even when asked, skilled pianists or organists seldom provide explanations that are particularly coherent.

Basically, for me, Bach's music oozes a sense of grace.

Week 2 explores grace through music. There are some interesting connections to be made. As with the illustrations in Week 1, it is not my own peculiar tastes that are important.

The theme of music, like that of family photographs, should allow you to provide your own particular examples instead. If Week 1 has been about visual expressions of grace, Week 2 is concerned more with aural expressions. And, having so far meditated mostly upon Mark, the meditations this week will be drawn from the psalms. Hearing grace in music.

As I write this, I have Bach's solo keyboard works playing in the background . . . just to remind me of how graceful they really are. Surprisingly, for those who know me, they are being played by András Schiff on a modern piano rather than on a traditional harpsichord or clavichord (the harpsichord plucks the notes, whereas the tiny clavichord hits them, but so quietly that only the musician can hear them properly). Twenty years ago I would have insisted upon a recording using a harpsichord (or perhaps a clavichord recorded with a microphone right next to it). After all, this is how Bach himself heard his music. Of course it may never be *exactly* how Bach heard it. There are obviously no direct recordings left by Bach and harpsichords and clavichords from the eighteenth century have been retuned, restrung and restored many times. We cannot possibly return to Bach's days, but (so I argued) we can at least get nearer to them by playing Bach on the sort of instruments that were around when Bach was alive.

Yet, several years of listening to and watching András Schiff's astonishingly sensitive playing at live concerts has changed me. Among Bach enthusiasts it is one of the great debates of the last three decades. Should Bach be played on 'authentic' instruments alone (including chamber organs) or upon modern instruments as well? In the sleeve notes that go with this particular Bach recording, András Schiff argues as follows:

I have great respect for 'authenticity' as such, but I must confess that the recorded Bach performances that have most moved me . . . have little to do with present-day scholarship, but they have all the more to do with general musicianship and great artistry – conveying the true spirit and grandeur of Bach. I have yet to hear a performance on original instruments that has evoked similar feelings or emotions in me.[1]

I am certainly not competent to engage in this argument. All that I have discovered from going to those concerts is that, for me at least, András Schiff's playing is almost as graceful as the music he plays. There is an elegance, energy and flow in his playing that helps me to hear and appreciate afresh the textures of Bach's keyboard music.

I remember one particularly graceful recital that he gave in the Usher Hall at the Edinburgh Festival. It started with the usual lecture from an administrator about the need for everyone to turn off mobile phones – a warning completely wasted on the non-English-speaking part of that international audience. This was followed by an abrupt halt at the end of the first piece. The same administrator returned to tell us that the BBC engineers recording the recital had detected a high-pitched noise from the audience. Sadly someone's hearing aid had been turned up too high.

After much shuffling, accusing looks and red faces, quiet was restored and the recital continued. Then, despite the incredibly uncomfortable seats and the heat from one of Edinburgh's rare moments of real summer, the multicultural audience became transfixed. Music through the fingers of a master player flowed across barriers of language and custom. András Schiff continues:

There are of course several ways of interpreting a masterpiece, and no solution is the only right one. Determining the tempo, for example, is one of the key points for any performance. There is not just one right tempo for any piece of music, but it is the performer's duty to present his tempo so convincingly that it will sound inevitable to the listener. The most miraculous thing about Bach's Preludes and Fugues is that you can play them convincingly in different tempi and with different articulation, dynamics, touch, phrasing – the greatness of the music will always shine through.

As an audience we were indeed convinced. Grace resounding around the Usher Hall.

———

MEDITATION
Psalm 150

8

Grace notes

In printed music grace notes are those tiny notes hanging in the air above the more solid notes. And they are played as fleeting embellishments. On the trumpet you just slip the valve, almost as if you didn't really intend to play the note at all, and move hurriedly on to the proper note. A grace note is a sort of extra note . . . a note for free ... gratis ... a little adornment . . . a passing note.

On a trumpet the odd grace note makes you sound like a considerably better player than you really are. Provided the grace note does not make fingering too difficult (definitely to be avoided on some combinations), it can really sound quite impressive. 'This person can really play' (when in reality grace notes can be quite easy). And they work just as well in baroque music as they do in jazz. Grace notes can add real zing to playing. And, sadly, they can also become quite tiresome. Too many grace notes in inappropriate places can soon pall.

Once again András Schiff sums up such musical embellishments well:

The understanding and use of ornaments, too, is another important ingredient of Bach interpretation. Ornamentation is as essential to music as it is to the visual arts and architecture. It would probably be very interesting to see a Gothic cathedral with just its plain walls, without ornaments, frescos and statues, but it would severely diminish our enjoyment and admiration of a great work of art. The important point in interpreting Bach is to decide where and when some form of ornamentation is needed or asked for.

There are many movements in Bach where one feels that a
simple treatment of the material is more appropriate, but to
evade the issue altogether is to ignore the essence of this era
of music – the joy of playing, discovering, improvising,
doing something unpredictable.

There are so many interesting ideas in this quotation that are
directly relevant to a sense of grace.

András Schiff uses the word 'feel'. Even he cannot really tell
us why he adds ornamentation in some parts of Bach's music
but not in others. Instead, he just writes that 'one feels that a
simple treatment' is the right one. There is something quite
intuitive about a sense of grace. Some moments in our lives,
some people, some places, some things, evoke in us a sense of
grace, whereas others do not. Essentially we are not in control
of grace. A sense of grace is evoked within us, triggered by certain key experiences and situations.

Again, András Schiff points to the similarities between
ornamentation in music and ornamentation in architecture. A
good part of my life is spent in Canterbury Cathedral. I have
been going to services perhaps once a week there for a dozen
years and yet every time I go there is something new to notice
about the building and its ornamentations and furniture.
There are even some features that I would never have noticed
at all if, after several years, I had not gone around with an
experienced guide. Then this year I went back to Guildford
Cathedral for evensong. It makes an astonishing contrast.
There are a few adornments on its walls (rather more than
when I was last there some 20 years ago) but not many.
For the most part it consists of huge unadorned pillars, walls
and windows looming without interruption. There is a great
sense of beauty in both buildings. A sense of grace can be quite
varied.

And then there is something quite elusive about ornamentation ... about grace. András Schiff writes as if his readers
were already aware that some of his playing of Bach includes

ornamentation and some does not. Whereas I suspect that many people will not even hear the ornamentation, and all the grace notes, at all. Because his playing is itself so graceful it feels almost crude to dissect his particular techniques. Like all true masters he can make it sound just so easy.

An academic friend once attended a small gathering at which the great Russian cellist Mstislav Rostropovich had played Bach cello suites. This was not a public concert but a very private and exclusive soirée. Rostropovich made the music and the playing sound so easy and fluent. Entranced, my clever but unmusical, friend rushed out afterwards and bought himself a cello. He too would learn to play these wonderful suites. Then, inevitably, he discovered that one of Rostropovich's elusive gifts was to make an exceedingly difficult instrument, playing music once thought to be quite unplayable, sound easy. Years and years of dedicated practice lay behind his great artistry. My friend never did learn to play that cello.

A sense of grace, too, can be elusive.

———◆———

MEDITATION
Psalm 103

9

Silent grace

Picking up an idea mentioned earlier, the word 'grace' can mean a pause, respite or reprieve. Students are always asking me for 'a bit of grace'. Of course what they are looking for is an extension of the date for submitting an essay. Perhaps other essays have accumulated, perhaps they have not been feeling too well, perhaps they are part-time students and have been busy at work, perhaps they are young parents with children to care for, or perhaps they have simply been to too many parties. Whatever. 'A bit of grace' is very popular when granted.

Pauses between sounds are as much a part of music as sound itself. For most of the time we pay little attention to this. We simply do not hear even the most dramatic pauses in music for what they are . . . space . . . silence. We are so bound up in the sound of the music that we do not notice fleeting, soundless moments of silence.

Perhaps to make this very point, one modern musician has composed a piece of music that is silent throughout. When performed, audiences are presumably given some indication of when it is to begin and when they might clap because it has ended. Yet in between there is nothing but silence. Some musical experts insist (I think seriously . . . but I am not entirely sure) that it is a genuine musical composition. Personally, I am glad that I have never actually attended a performance. I simply cannot imagine an audience keeping entirely quiet and still while it is 'played'. Why is it that many of us suddenly develop an overwhelming urge to cough and splutter whenever communal silence is required? And even the slightest background noise becomes magnified many times over in those moments of shared 'silence'.

Breaking through the moment of stillness, recently, following my final Blessing a three-year-old girl's voice could be heard by the whole congregation asking, 'Can we go now?'

As a young student at theological college I was required to take part in communal retreats. Some students really valued them and returned for retreats at the same place for many years after being ordained. Unfortunately, because they were so strictly enforced, I regarded them as acts of penance to be endured rather than enjoyed. For two or three days we were not allowed to talk to our friends, even though we continued to eat, relax, study and pray together. Childishly we developed elaborate forms of sign language, especially at the meal table. We tried not to play jokes on each other and failed. We even played silent croquet. For me, at least, this enforced silence simply became oppressive.

Yet moments of silence *are* essential in music. To demonstrate this one gifted musician illustrated a lecture by playing the familiar Beethoven piano piece, 'Für Elise' – a favourite of many budding pianists. The first time he played it with a completely regular beat and with little or no intervals between the different phrases. It sounded simply appalling. In fact it sounded just like the deliberately infuriating signal on the fire alarm in my house. And then he played it with tiny intervals (that he invited us to listen to) and varying silent gaps between the phrases. Now it sounded like genuine music. The difference was not in the actual notes that he played, but in the silent spaces that he left between them.

Silence is also invaluable within prayer. Although I still do not cope particularly well with communal silence, I have learned to treasure it within prayer on my own. Much private prayer tends to be articulated in the form of words. Perhaps they are the formal and elegant words of the 1662 Prayer Book or the less stilted words of modern Prayer Books. Perhaps, instead, they are the spontaneous words of everyday conversation, albeit addressed to God rather than to other people. The way that we use words in private prayer can be very varied. Yet, for me, words can become a great hindrance within prayer. Because so much of my academic life is spent analysing words, especially the various words used to articulate religious faith, I do not always find them particularly helpful within private prayer. For me, at least, music can be a more helpful medium for prayer. And silence can be even more helpful.

There is the silence of the summer evening as thrushes finish singing and before owls start hooting and whistling. There is the silence of the winter night watching embers glow in a dying fire. There is the silence while walking along a riverbank between autumn rainstorms. There is the silence of the wind in early spring on a deserted beach or on an open moor. There is the silence of snowflakes falling on a white garden or of trees covered in hoar frost. There is the silence of water on a calm lake. There is the silence of a well-fed baby sleeping.

Silence evoking a sense of grace.

———◆◆———

MEDITATION
Psalm 131

10

Pomp and grace

Music can also be excellent at poking fun at pomposity. People who have too high an opinion of themselves – who put on 'airs and graces' – have often been on the receiving end of witty composers.

For several years I played French horn or trumpet (according to need) in local productions of Gilbert and Sullivan. Up to that point I had had no interest at all in their work. Like many people I had simply missed their gentle humour and parody. Then playing night after night in one work after another I began to catch the bug. Music and words are so well matched together, pricking the bubbles of the pompous – in the army, in government, in the law courts and in the church as well. Our local MP often played trumpet, too, and occasionally joined the parody with a walk-on part as a politician.

Gilbert and Sullivan works are splendid for semi-competent musicians such as myself. When I first started playing in their works I used to count every bar. For a brass player this can be quite hard work, since there are long sections without brass instruments playing at all. Then a more experienced player showed me how to distinguish the different sections (they are usually written to a formula) without counting at all. At last I was free to listen to the words of the singers instead. Now I really could hear the wonderful combination of deliberately pompous words with equally pompous music.

Brass players are not always very popular with singers in amateur productions. The trouble is that we misguidedly tend to believe that audiences have come to hear us and not the singers. That, of course, may just be the case for the loved ones that we drag along (although even that is dubious), but it is certainly not true for anyone else. Left to their own devices, many singers would probably ban us altogether. However, Gilbert and Sullivan without at least the occasional blast on a trumpet or hunting call on the French horn would soon lack its wonderful airs and graces. So there is typically an uneasy truce between the singers and the brass section. They do need each other, but they would rather not.

In the phrase 'airs and graces' the term 'graces' suggests, perhaps, someone who engages in pretentious embellishments. If embellishments can, as seen earlier, add to the enjoyment of some styles of music, they can also easily be overdone. Sullivan's music knows exactly how to do that. At many points his music offers us a purposefully exaggerated rendering of the 'serious' opera of his day. And then he lets the chorus echo the exaggerated words that Gilbert, in turn, has given to a principal singer.

Such deliberate and pretentious embellishments have also characterized many famous paintings of the self-important. There are those wonderful portraits of the nobility or wealthy gentry by artists such as Reynolds or Gainsborough, with their fine clothes and haughty looks. There are the cartoons of Hogarth, even more obviously making fun of the rich and powerful. And there are satirists today embellishing some embarrassing feature of modern celebrities in order to ridicule them. 'Graces' understood in this sense act as a sharp reminder to us when we are tempted to be pretentious.

Every summer at Leeds Castle in Kent there are open-air concerts together with firework displays. From our house on the North Downs we always know when the '1812 Overture' is being played as the climax to the programme. The sky lights up with the fireworks and the cannons punctuate the distant music. Several thousand people attend these popular concerts. They come armed with huge picnic hampers, deckchairs and even tables. These all have to be carried, hours before the concert starts, a good half-mile across the grass in order to book a space for the evening. People drink, eat and sing along to the music, with the beautiful castle and lake illuminated in the background.

This is not an event for musical snobs. People in the audience wave Union Jacks, Scottish and Welsh Flags and occasionally even European Union Flags. It is a display of eccentric Britishness, with pockets of French, German, American and even somewhat bemused Japanese visitors as well. Overwhelmingly it is premised upon self-parody.

As darkness descends the music becomes ever more 'patriotic'. 'Pomp and Circumstance', 'Land of Hope and Glory', 'Rule Britannia', the lot. However, a few individuals in the audience refuse to join in. It is easy to see why. Displays of Prom-type patriotism can be highly offensive to some. So they sit silently on their deckchairs with arms folded while everyone around them is singing and cheering. I suspect they have missed the self-parody. This is an audience making fun of itself. It is an audience using this musical occasion to mock the pretensions of past, imperial history. I doubt if it is really an attempt to relive that history.

Airs and graces depicted in music.

———◆◆◆———

MEDITATION
Psalm 81

11

A song of grace

Music and singing seem to have had a central place in worship throughout history. For some reason, when people come together to worship, we usually expect to sing or, at least, to listen to singing on our behalf. In most services we also need to have music in some form. It is really difficult to explain why.

It is probably a mistake to offer an explanation. Singing is typically something that we do together, and we are embarrassed if we are caught singing in the bath or the shower. Across many different cultures and religions people gather together to sing and feel strangely uplifted when they do so. Singing in church seems to stem from that collective feeling. Most of us can express a sense of grace more readily through poetry and singing than we can through prose.

The Jewish Psalms used this week in the meditations are an important reminder of the power of singing and music within worship. Among scholars there has been much discussion over the last century about the relationship of the Psalms to Jewish worship. There are frequent mentions of both singing and music within the Psalms themselves, as well as references to worship:

> O come, let us sing to the Lord;
> let us make a joyful noise to the rock of our salvation!
> Let us come into his presence with thanksgiving;
> let us make a joyful noise to him with songs of praise . . .
> O come, let us worship and bow down,
> let us kneel before the Lord, our Maker! (Psalm 95.1–2, 6)

O sing to the Lord a new song;
sing to the Lord, all the earth.
Sing to the Lord, bless his name;
tell of his salvation from day to day. (Psalm 96.1–2)

Praise him with trumpet sound;
praise him with lute and harp!
Praise him with tambourine and dance;
praise him with strings and pipe!
Praise him with loud clashing cymbals!
Let everything that breathes praise the Lord!
Praise the Lord! (Psalm 150.3–6)

Such verses do suggest that the Psalms are not simply ancient poems but actually survivors of a long-lost tradition of cultic music as well.

The Jewish Psalms are now, of course, shared by Christians as well. Indeed, in the seventeenth and early eighteenth centuries, psalms and paraphrases of psalms were the only form of singing allowed in many churches and chapels. Hymns as we know them today only became fashionable towards the end of the eighteenth century (Week 4 will return to this theme). Despite blunt expressions of violence and vengeance in some of the Psalms (often put in brackets in older prayer books), the Psalter was for a long time the staple diet of Christian worship.

Among the riches of the Psalms, there is one that has been particularly linked with a sense of grace. It is the psalm printed in the Bible as two separate psalms, 42 and 43. Most scholars today believe that the two form a single whole. This combined psalm opens with one of the most endearing images in the Psalter:

As a deer longs for flowing streams,
so my soul longs for you, O God.
My soul thirsts for God,
for the living God.

The seventeenth-century paraphrase, still sung in many churches, has shaped interpretations of this psalm. It adds a fanciful touch to the original in the second line and then makes an explicit reference to grace in the fourth line:

> As pants the hart for cooling streams
> When heated in the chase,
> So longs my soul, O God, for thee,
> And thy refreshing grace.

The psalm itself continues:

> My tears have been my food
> day and night,
> while people say to me continually,
> 'Where is your God?'

This theme of personal desolation keeps recurring in verses that follow: 'My soul is cast down within me'; 'Why are you cast down, O my soul, and why are you so disquieted within me?' (twice); and 'Why must I walk about mournfully because of the oppression of the enemy?'

Yet between these moments of desolation, there is another, quite different, note. At three crucial stages of the combined psalm the same words occur:

> Hope in God; for I shall again praise him,
>   my help and my God

Despite the immense difficulties of translating psalms from their original Hebrew into English (difficulties that account for the many variations in wording from one English version to another), it is possible to hear another note. Even if the original Hebrew cadences and melodies have been lost, this psalm in particular can still evoke a sense of poetry and music.

In turn, this can evoke a sense of grace. It will be seen later that this typically begins with an awareness of human frailty, before moving to a sense of God's help or grace. Despite feeling so 'cast down', the writer (whether living in exile, as some have speculated, or just temporarily away from home) still remembers that:

By day the Lord commands his steadfast love,
and at night his song is with me,
a prayer to the God of my life.

A song of grace.

———◆———

MEDITATION
Psalms 42 and 43

12

Different graces

Sometime sung and sometimes spoken,
usually in English, but occasionally in Latin,
on formal occasions in banquets,
at informal family gatherings,
even at times in secular society
Grace is offered before eating together.

Of course meal-time grace was more common in the past. Yet it is remarkable that it still survives today. Standing to attention for the National Anthem at the end of a cinema programme has long gone. Yet meal-time grace, on occasions, remains.

Inevitably, being ordained, I am often asked to 'say grace' on public occasions ('Padre, will you do the grace?'). I frequently struggle with this. Some believe that this is an occasion to proclaim an unambiguous Christian faith. I can see why they believe that. I can also see why some are convinced that this simply antagonizes doubters . . . another nail in the Christian coffin. I also have considerable sympathy for faithful Jews and Muslims, who share a common faith in God to whom they wish to give thanks, but not a faith in Jesus as Son of God. As a result, I attempt to be as inclusive as possible in public graces.

Some manage to do this with wit as well. At a banquet given by the Bible Society to a very high ranking (and largely secular) delegation of Chinese government officials, the Bishop of London, Richard Chartres, was asked to say the grace. He had listened to the initial speeches in which delegates had thanked the hosts, referring to themselves jocularly as 'big potatoes' meeting other 'big potatoes'. So the bishop lightened what could have been an awkward grace by thanking God both for the food and for the 'big potatoes' present. The Chinese officials beamed approval. A more conventional grace might not have worked so well.

When visiting the Anglican church in Grahamstown, South Africa, I collected another Michael Ramsey story to add to my collection (it is an occupational hazard that goes with my particular job). During a rather stormy visit to South Africa in the days of apartheid, Archbishop Ramsey stayed the night at the local theological college. The theological students were thrilled at the prospect of meeting the great man. For many of them this was the one and only occasion that they saw his familiar face in the flesh, with the huge bald head and sprigs of white hair going in all directions, the twinkling eyes and disengaged smile. He rolled rather than walked and always looked vaguely lost. A benign, clever, spiritual and other-worldly figure.

One of the students was asked to say grace before dinner. Completely overawed by the occasion, he blurted out: 'The grace of our Lord Jesus Christ, the love of God, and the fellowship of the Holy Spirit, be always with you.' There was a stunned silence. Then His Grace's shoulders began to heave and everyone laughed. Tension was broken.

Saying or singing grace is a way of giving thanks to God the creator and sustainer of the world. In former times it might also have been a way of giving thanks to God for the specific weather conditions requested in prayer to grow that particular food. For most of us in the modern world there is seldom such a direct connection between the food we eat, our own physical labour and local weather conditions. Buying food from supermarkets it may take an act of imagination to think of it being grown at all.

In any case, there always were problems about asking God to produce particular local weather conditions. Given our (somewhat) better understanding of global weather patterns, a local condition requested here may well affect weather conditions for worse halfway around the world. Anyway, specific weather suitable for our vegetables might be disastrous for our neighbour's different vegetables. And, quite apart from all of that, such an understanding of God – interfering with the local weather – does seem to be at odds with the God of freedom made known in Jesus.

By singing or saying grace before special meals we join a long religious tradition of praise going back at least as far as the Psalms: 'Make a joyful noise to the Lord, all the earth. Worship the Lord with gladness; come into his presence with singing' (Psalm 100.1–2); 'The Lord is king! Let the earth rejoice: let the many coastlands be glad' (Psalm 97.1); 'May God be gracious to us and bless us and make his face to shine upon us' (Psalm 67.1); 'The earth is the Lord's and all that is in it, the world, and those who live in it' (Psalm 24.1).

We also make a connection between faith and food. Many religious traditions make some connection. Some prohibit eating certain types of food – pork for Jews and Muslims, beef for Hindus. Many make some positive connection between food and worship. For Jews it is the Passover meal shared by families. For Christians it is the Eucharist.

A connection, if you will, between food and grace.

MEDITATION
Psalm 24

38

WEEK 3

There But For Grace

------◆------

13

Far from grace

A sense of grace – a sense of God's help in our lives – starts with an awareness of personal frailty. As long as we imagine that we can be good on our own and without any divine help, then we are unlikely to know anything about grace. Sometimes we need to confront evil even to see the need for grace.

This week we will explore the bleak theme of evil and suffering through stories in the news and with meditations from Job. Together they illustrate the saying, often attributed to the sixteenth century martyr, John Bradford. Seeing a group of criminals being led to their execution, he is supposed to have remarked, 'There but for the grace of God, go I.' Later, when Mary Tudor became queen, he was himself burnt alive at Smithfield.

One of the most disturbing programmes that I have ever seen on television was called: 'Iceman: Confessions of a Mafia Hitman'. It told the apparently true story of the Mafia hitman, Richard Kuklinski. The programmers interviewed him in the prison cell in the United States where he is currently serving a life sentence, with little prospect of ever being released. He may have committed as many as 200 murders.

He told the interviewer how he had first become a Mafia hitman. Having already committed murder as a young man, he had discovered that he actually found pleasure in killing people efficiently (as a child he had tortured animals). The local Mafia soon noticed his 'skills' and, in turn, he volunteered his services to them. Apparently he combined the attributes of a sociopath (killing without remorse) with the secrecy of one brought up without love in a violent household – a rare and deadly combination.

Speaking in a quiet and pleasant voice, he told the story about the initial test he faced before being offered the job. The Mafia boss drove him to a quiet road and stopped the car. Pointing to a complete stranger out walking his dog, the Mafia boss simply ordered Kuklinski to murder him. Richard Kuklinski climbed out of the car, walked quietly up behind the stranger, shot him dead, and then got back into the car. As a result he got the job. He had proved to his new boss that he could murder an innocent stranger efficiently and without emotion. Because of his secretive nature, he was also able to do so without being detected – he did not feel a need to brag to others afterwards.

Richard Kuklinski took great pride in murder. He liked to devise novel and ingenious ways of committing murder efficiently and without detection. Sometimes he took considerable trouble to work out the best way of murdering someone in public without getting caught. He regarded this as a skill to be refined and enjoyed. Occasionally he murdered people for personal reasons. He was quite prepared to murder one of his few friends and, perhaps predictably, eventually murdered his boss. Yet, for the most part, he was murdering people impersonally and dispassionately on instructions from the Mafia. This was his job and apparently he relished it.

At the time of the television interview he had already been in prison for a decade. Now in his sixties he expressed no remorse for any of his murders. For him it was just a job and he boasted he had been good at it. Asked whether he would still do it, he responded that he was now too old. To murder people efficiently you needed to be agile. A large and now lumbering man, he no longer considered he had the necessary speed. And, in any case, having murdered no one for a decade, he had lost the sense of thrill that such murders once gave him. Carefully crafted and executed killing no longer excited him.

Of course I have no idea whether or not Richard Kuklinski was exaggerating or even fantasizing. This was after all a television programme. Perhaps beneath the bravado he was a thoroughly remorseful human being, wracked with guilt about the people he had murdered and the families he had left bereaved. Perhaps. Yet at face value, the programme suggested otherwise. What was deeply disturbing was the suggestion that someone, apparently so ordinary and well-mannered, could murder dozens of people because he found it pleasurable. For him murder seemed to consist of nothing more than something he was good at doing.

Thank God few of us will share his pleasure at efficient and undetected murder. However the very fact that many of us do find such a programme intriguing suggests that we know something of the attraction of evil. Of course we normally strip this attraction of any relationship to the real world. The whodunnit detective novel or film allows us to fantasize about efficient and undetected murder without having to cope with the emotions of real people. The genre permits us to be fascinated with such murder in the abstract. Shockingly, the interview with Richard Kuklinski appeared to be reality. Yet television programmers were well aware that many 'ordinary' people would also find it fascinating.

It is our capacity to be fascinated by evil that tells us something both about ourselves and about evil itself. Richard Kuklinski is different from most of us, but there are also features we share with him. Murder evidently gave him power over others and a strong sense of personal importance.

A Sense of Grace

Murder offered him an opportunity to experiment and innovate regardless of the effect on other people. Murder provided him with an easy and well-paid life. We can all identify with much of this. And each of these features suggests that evil is seductive.

There is something disturbingly seductive and fascinating about someone so far from grace.

———•◆•———

MEDITATION
Job 2.1–13

14

Lost grace

Another television programme, but this time about a British prisoner. Andrew Aston is serving a record 26 life terms for two murders and 26 assaults on elderly people.

To feed his hard-drug dependency, Andrew Aston knocked on the doors of the frail elderly posing (rather improbably) as a plain-clothes policeman. Once inside their homes, he demanded money threatening violence. Shockingly, even when had been given the money, he then assaulted these old people viciously and gratuitously, killing two of them in the process and leaving others badly injured. Once established as a suspect, police had only to follow him along the street before he knocked on someone's door and gained entry. Acting quickly, they managed to arrest him just before he claimed a twenty-seventh victim.

All of this was reconstructed for television viewers. Then extracts from the real-life videotapes of him being interviewed in the police station were shown. Despite the large amount of evidence gathered by the police, and despite being in prison before for violent crime, he flatly denied any violent or criminal behaviour. He claimed that he had never been violent to anyone. Even when confronted with his police record, he continued to deny everything.

Much of the programme focused on his father, Roger Aston. He had apparently agreed to take an active part in the programme in order to establish why his son had done these terrible acts of violence against vulnerable, old people. A highly distressing family background emerged. On his own admission, Roger Aston was a promiscuous alcoholic who had deserted his family. He had regularly used corporal punishment on his son when young (but not on his daughter) and explained, 'I needed to make him cry . . . so he would know I had ownership over him'. If the young boy did not cry when he first hit him, he would just hit harder. Eventually the son learned how to provoke his father still further. He would tell lies habitually, knowing that this particularly angered his father, and then he would stop himself crying even when his father punished him by hitting him as hard as he could. In turn, when he became an adult, Andrew Aston assaulted both his father and his mother.

Deserted by her husband, Andrew Aston's mother found that once Andrew was an adolescent she could no longer cope with his increasing violence. He had also become a drug addict and regularly stole her money to pay for the drugs. So she locked him out of the home. For a time he lived uneasily with his father and his father's new wife. Then he left them and drifted further into drug-addiction and violent crime.

The implication of the programme was clear. Andrew Aston's appalling crimes were the product of a broken home and a violent upbringing. However there were also hints that this explanation was too simple. A relative recalled that Roger Aston's mother had deeply loved her young grandson and that he had responded warmly to this love. He was not remembered at school as being especially difficult or violent. And the pattern of youthful rebellion did not appear to everyone interviewed as especially unusual. After all, many other young people are brought up in broken and sometimes violent homes, yet they do not viciously attack old people. Again, there is a great deal of violent crime associated with hard-drug dependency, but the pattern of murder and violence for which Andrew Aston was convicted is fortunately rare.

So why did he do it? Neither Roger Aston nor the programme itself seemed able to give a satisfactory answer. The father (and implicitly the programme) partly blamed himself. However he concluded that, although he still loved him, Andrew probably should never have been born and (chillingly) should now be hanged for his crimes.

The awareness of personal frailty that precedes a sense of grace often contains three elements – blame, self-blame and sheer bewilderment. Andrew's difficult background must have contributed something to his appalling crimes. He is manifestly a deeply damaged individual. There is an enormous amount of research showing that a stable and loving family life is very important for producing good citizens. Nonetheless to blame everything on his family is simply to miss the obvious point that few others from similar backgrounds resort to such serious crime.

At some point, it could be argued, Andrew Aston must have known that what he was doing was seriously wrong, if not evil. He had known love from his grandmother and yet (doubtless distorted by drugs), he had remorselessly beaten other people's grandmothers. How could he not know that this was wrong?

Yet sheer bewilderment also remains. This especially brutal behaviour deeply shocked those involved in his trial. Evil had become so deeply seductive that a boy, who had once known grace from an elderly person, had now come to show no mercy whatsoever to other elderly people.

Evil overwhelming grace.

MEDITATION
Job 3.1–16

15

The two graces

The sculptor Antonio Canova created his masterpiece *The Three Graces* between 1815 and 1817. Carved in white marble, it depicts the three Greek goddesses of beauty. The three life-size figures are locked together in a circle, facing inwards and permanently embracing each other. Now on display alternately at the National Gallery of Scotland in Edinburgh and the Victoria and Albert Museum in London, visitors are encouraged to walk right round the sculpture gazing on the soft and elegant lines. Despite the coldness and hardness of the marble, we see instead the soft, warm flesh of the three intertwined figures.

Laleh and Ladan Bijani were joined together for all but the last few minutes of their lives. Fused together towards the back of their heads, for 29 years the Iranian sisters could only look on the face of their twin through a mirror. Although they longed to be separate from each other, they had no choice but to do everything together. As children they played together and then tried to run in separate directions, only to collapse in pain. And as adults they would have liked to have studied quite different subjects but, in the end, did law at university together and even received a joint degree (examiners found it impossible to prevent them sharing information). They had very different interests and hobbies – one loved computer games and the other hated them – yet, whatever they wanted, they simply had to be with each other at all times.

Other twins will know something about the intimacy of sharing early life closely with another, of sharing prams and toys and, of course, birthdays. Many identical twins dress alike from choice and enjoy confusing strangers. Whether identical or not, twins frequently share jokes and invented words and remain bonded for life in a way that seems odd to others. We are an unusual group.

However, only those conjoined twins who cannot be separated when young can know what it is like to be truly inseparable. For Laleh and Ladan this became torture. They longed to lead separate lives and were finally prepared to undergo a lengthy, complex and extremely dangerous operation in the hope that this might allow them to do so. In the event, as we all know, the operation killed them and they were unconscious even for their final, brief moment of separated life.

Newspapers were obsessed with these two young graces as they prepared for their operation. There were pictures of them driving a car together, saying prayers together as faithful Muslims, and laughing as they took an automatic photograph of themselves. In Iran and then, in their last few months, in Singapore waiting for their operation, they were treated as celebrities. Apparently, even though the public stared at them as they shopped or walked in the street, the twins responded with warmth and humour.

But they lacked the one thing that almost everyone else in the world takes for granted – the capacity to be on their own. Other twins, with our curious intimacy, still have that capacity. It is only when we see someone with a serious disability, that we start to fantasize about what life must be like without something that we otherwise take for granted. We see life differently. Indeed, we normally think that it is a compliment to say that a couple are 'inseparable'. Clearly not for Laleh and Ladan. Disability and innocent suffering can indeed evoke in us a sense of 'there but for the grace of God, go I'.

When Laleh and Ladan Bijani died there was a vexed debate about whether or not it had been right to attempt to do the operation at all. Some had claimed initially that the odds of success were about even. In the event others calculated the chances of success for adults joined at the head to be separated, successfully and without brain damage to one or other of the twins, was nearer to 5 per cent. Yet, however calculated, the twins themselves were intelligent and educated adults who must have been aware of the real danger they faced.

Some maintained that doctors should never proceed with such risky operations. It is the role of doctors to benefit patients, not to risk excessive harm against them. Yet, if pressed, this argument would disallow many novel forms of treatment. For example, the first heart transplants brought little benefit to the patients involved, even though they have brought enormous benefit to others later. Again, some maintained that risky operations on those whose lives are not actually at risk are wrong. This is an important point, but it is still not conclusive. Laleh and Ladan believed that their lives together were so unbearable that they were ready to take the risk. As it happens, the unusual pressure within their conjoined skulls may also have been causing them acute pain and real danger.

Rightly or wrongly the operation went ahead and they died. Pictures showed their separate coffins draped in flowers and cloth, waiting in a mosque to return home for burial. The twins had been separated, as they had wished but not in the way that they had hoped and prayed. In their last moments of consciousness before their anaesthetic they read from the Koran. Doubtless, as dutiful Muslims, they prayed for grace – for God's help in their lives.

———•◆•———

MEDITATION
Job 10.1–22

16

Blind grace

Confronted with serious disability, many of us have a strong feeling of 'there but for the grace of God, go I'. The theologian John Hull has done more than most to challenge this.

As a young lecturer in religious education at Birmingham University he was sighted, but wore very thick glasses and held books close to his eyes. Over the years, his sight faded. At one point he was no longer able to read, but could still see shapes. Eventually he lost even these shapes. Now he sees nothing.

In time he became a professor and an established, international expert in his field. However, through his writings on disability and the many interviews he has given to journalists and television programme makers, he has become known to a much wider public. With a mixture of wit and wisdom he has communicated to the sighted something of what it means to be blind.

In his earliest writings after becoming blind, he helped sighted readers to understand the transition he faced. For a while he still thought as a sighted person himself. His mental images were drawn from sight and he lived and worked as one deprived of sight. Then slowly this began to change. His memories of sight grew weaker and new children were born whom he would never see. His relationship with them was based upon touch, sound and smell rather than upon sight. On one occasion he was 'reading' a bed-time story to his young son and had forgotten to turn on the light. The child innocently imagined that his father uniquely had the ability to read in the dark. In a sense he did.

When it was wet, he now stopped trying to imagine the sight of rain. Instead, he listened to the different sounds of rain beating against roofs, windows and paths and smelt rain mingling with the pebbles, grass and flowers. He began to think of himself, less as one who had lost sight, and more as a person with other senses. Being clever and ingenious, he established an office in the university with advanced computer equipment to allow him to 'read' books and not to rely upon others reading to him. And like many blind people, he learned the contours and sounds of the pavements that he walked every day to and from the university.

Of course there were still frustrations. I never remember his study in the university being particularly tidy. Like the rest of us, I suspect he was always losing things in the deluge of papers that make up the academic life. Without sight, searching for lost books and papers must now have become even more difficult and irritating. However his humour and enthusiasm for his subject and students remain very much intact.

In his more recent writings he has explored images of blindness in the Bible. He helps sighted people to realize that, taken at face value, they are manifestly written by other sighted people. Again and again, biblical authors use 'blindness' (and 'deafness') as a metaphor for spiritual failure:

They shall see the glory of the Lord,
the majesty of our God . . .
Then the eyes of the blind shall be opened,
and the ears of the deaf unstopped. (Isaiah 35.2 and 5)

I am the Lord, I have called you in righteousness,
I have taken you by the hand and kept you;
I have given you as a covenant to the people,
a light to the nations,
to open the eyes that are blind. (Isaiah 42.6–7)

Even the Gospels tend to contrast 'blindness' negatively with 'sight', and 'darkness' negatively with 'light':

Your eye is the lamp of your body. If your eye is healthy, your whole body is full of light; but if it is not healthy, your body is full of darkness. Therefore consider whether the light in you is not darkness. (Luke 11.34–35)

And several of the healing stories in the Gospels involve blind people being enabled to 'see' once more. Mark's story of 'blind' Bartimaeus is typical:

So throwing off his cloak, he sprang up and came to Jesus. Then Jesus said to him, 'What do you want me to do for you?' The blind man said to him, 'My teacher, let me see again.' Jesus said to him, 'Go; your faith has made you well.' Immediately he regained his sight and followed him on the way. (Mark 10.50–52)

In contrast, John Hull invites those of us who are sighted to consider these stories from his perspective and to be more cautious about negative images of 'blindness'. It was only once he had been able to move to a more positive understanding of blindness, that he was finally able to stop pining for a sense he would never regain.

The feeling of 'there but for the grace of God, go I' is only the first stage in a sense of grace. Eventually it needs to be overcome. It is only too natural for those of us who are sighted to feel it when confronted with those who are not. Grace lies in going beyond this.

Perhaps even discovering grace in blindness.

MEDITATION
Job 29.1–15

17

Suffering grace

I have just listened to a deeply moving radio programme about Edith Stein. Some suffering is caused by our genes or our birth. However there is also much suffering that is deliberately inflicted by human beings upon each other.

Edith Stein was born to a German Jewish family in 1891. She was exceedingly bright and studied at university under one of Germany's leading philosophers of the time. By the time she was 30 she had already become quite famous herself as a philosopher. Some scholars still judge her to be one of the most remarkable women philosophers of the twentieth century, developing radical ideas that the novelist and philosopher Jean-Paul Sartre was later to popularize.

In 1922 she became a Roman Catholic. As a result she worked hard to bring together the ideas she had developed as a secular philosopher with ideas she inherited from her new-found Christian faith. The work of the greatest medieval theologian (and perhaps the greatest theologian of all time) Thomas Aquinas was particularly attractive to her. Working now as a Christian philosopher, she sought to show that Aquinas was still relevant in the modern world.

Then, in 1934, at the age of 43, she made another radical change. She became a Carmelite nun. As the radio programme pointed out, the Carmelites are a deeply ascetic order, devoted to a life of prayer. Whereas other religious orders for women have a strong commitment to teaching, nursing or social work, Carmelites seek to serve the church and wider society through prayer and contemplation. The regime within her convent in the Netherlands was strict. Nuns were only allowed one short visit a month and, even then, talked with family visitors from behind a metal grille. The programme suggested that this must have been particularly difficult for her Jewish family. Not only had Edith Stein left her family faith, but she had chosen to be treated almost like a prisoner as well.

In the early 1940s the Nazis occupied the Netherlands and began their brutal purge against Dutch Jews. The story was told on the programme of how the Dutch Catholic bishops agonized about how they should respond. Courageously they decided to defy the Nazis and publicly denounced their evil programme of Jewish deportation. The Nazis were furious and swiftly took revenge. They decreed that even Jewish people who had converted to Christianity were to be deported along with all other Jews. Soon they came to the Carmelite convent and demanded that Edith Stein should be handed over to them. The nuns there were distraught and shrieked in anger. In the traumatic scenes that followed Edith Stein remained calm, believing that it was proper that she and her sister Rosa should join their own people in their fate. They were transported like cattle to Auschwitz in 1942 and, like millions of others, probably gassed on arrival.

The Nazi Holocaust remains one of the most shameful acts of western 'civilization'. Millions of the Jewish people – along with the Romany people, Jehovah's Witness members and people with learning disabilities – were murdered by the Nazis. To do this the Nazis systematically used modern technology and bureaucracy – the very means used to create the wealth supporting western 'civilization'. The Holocaust depended upon these western achievements to build the concentration camps and gas-chambers and to organize and sustain the efficient disposal of so many human beings. The architects of the Holocaust, acting together, were as efficient and dispassionate as Richard Kuklinski was later to be acting on his own. They had developed an impersonal and effective way of murdering millions of clever people without too many of their neighbours objecting.

The Holocaust also depended upon a western culture –

shamefully, including the churches – that had long carried
images of anti-Semitism. Visitors to Strasbourg Cathedral, for
instance, can see this for themselves. On either side of the
great southern entrance to the cathedral are two finely carved
thirteenth-century statues of women. The one on the left
depicts the church. Holding a victorious cross with one hand
and a chalice with the other, she looks triumphantly across to
the figure opposite. The statue on the right represents the synagogue. She is a defeated and more lascivious figure, looking
downwards in defeat. Carved at a time of fierce medieval anti-
Semitism in Europe, they remain stark and permanent
reminders of a legacy that ended in the Holocaust.

It is a legacy we would probably rather forget today. Edith
Stein is a sharp reminder. A gifted western philosopher murdered by a heartless western power solely because she had
been born into a Jewish family. A Christian nun dispassionately gassed by a culture long shaped by Christian values. A
human being persecuted pointlessly by her fellow human
beings . . . there but for the grace of God . . .

> and Edith Stein herself
> calmly going to her death at Auschwitz
> in the hope of grace beyond death.

MEDITATION
Job 38.1–17

18

Grace through frailty

The intriguing book of Job from which all of the meditations this week have been taken, has long been recognized as one of the great masterpieces of the Jewish Bible. Yet it has also puzzled Jews and Christians alike for centuries.

For linguists who know the original Hebrew, the prologue, in the first two chapters, and the epilogue, in the final chapter, are quite different from the central part of Job (3.1—42.4). As can be detected from the lay-out in many modern English versions, the prologue and epilogue are in prose, whereas the rest is in verse. The prologue and epilogue also contain many unique words from a mixture of Hebrew, Aramaic and Arabic. Even the ideas they contain (such as the patience of Job) are sometimes at odds with those in the central part (where Job is anything but patient).

Like many classic sagas and poems, Job has been interpreted quite differently by people over the centuries and within varying cultures. For some modern Jewish writers it is, not surprisingly, a depiction of persecution likened to the Holocaust, whereas for others it portrays personal grief or psychological anxiety. For many Christians it wrestles with the so-called problem of evil – of why a loving God allows innocent suffering in the world. However, in a tradition going back at least to Augustine, it is also an account of a path towards grace.

It is not difficult to see why Christians have seen Job in terms of such a path. It contains two essential features of a sense of grace that will be explored further next week: a growing awareness of personal frailty and a corresponding sense of the mystery of God.

An awareness of personal frailty is a recurrent theme in Job. The three 'friends' of Job – Eliphaz the Temanite, Bildad the Shuhite, and Zophar the Naamathite – constantly nag him about his frailty as a human being and about his sinfulness. Eliphaz opens the attack with the obsequious words: 'If one ventures a word with you, will you be offended?' Why is it that 'friends' always use such a phrase when they are just about to be really offensive? Very soon the rudeness starts:

> 'Call now; is there anyone who will answer you?
> To which of the holy ones will you turn?
> Surely vexation kills the fool,
> and jealousy slays the simple.' (Job 5.1–2)

'Fool', 'simple', 'jealousy' . . . the compliments keep being hurled at poor Job. In turn, he keeps protesting his own innocence and outrage at the fact that the wicked prosper. An unhealthy, but all too understandable, mixture of self-righteousness and indignation. For good measure, he also reminds his 'friends' that, 'Those who withhold kindness from a friend forsake the fear of the Almighty' (6.14).

Alongside this there are also numerous references by Job to his own wretched condition, longing at times that he had never been born:

> 'Let the day perish in which I was born,
> and the night that said,
> "A man-child is conceived."
> Let that day be darkness!' (3.3–4)

Then, halfway through Job there is a beautiful poetic interlude. The complaints and bitterness stop and there is a sudden glimpse of the glory and mystery of God's wisdom. A search is made for wisdom in the mines of gold, silver and precious stones, but wisdom is not found there. Nor can wisdom be bought with great riches. Rather it is God alone who understands the way of wisdom and it is God who says to humankind:

> 'Truly, the fear of the Lord, that is wisdom;
> And to depart from evil is understanding.' (28.28)

Yet immediately after this chapter the self-righteousness and indignation of Job himself continue. Readers have to wait for another ten chapters before the voice of God returns:

> Then the Lord answered Job out of the whirlwind:
> 'Who is this that darkens counsel by words without
>   knowledge?
> Gird up your loins like a man,
> I will question you, and you shall declare to me.
> Where were you when I laid the foundations of the earth?
> Tell me, if you have understanding.
> Who determined its measurements – surely you know!
> Or who stretched the line upon it?' (38.1–5)

For four chapters Job is challenged by God. As a mere human being, does Job really know what is involved in God creating the world? Finally overawed, Job admits that, 'I have uttered what I did not understand, things too wonderful for me, which I did not know' (42.3).

Confronted with human frailty, pain and suffering, it is only too natural for us to ask, 'Why should a loving God allow this?' Perhaps we should sometimes also ask, 'Could the world really have been otherwise?' We readily assume that God could have made a world of real freedom and moral choice without any accompanying pain or suffering. We assume that but, without being God, how do we know that such a world is really possible? Perhaps it is possible to have a world without real freedom and moral choice that also lacks pain and suffering. Yet that would be a world fit for machines not for people. Could a world fit for people really have been otherwise?

Job finally reaches a point of grace. He finds humility. And, with this humility, comes a sense of 'things too wonderful for me'.

———◆———

MEDITATION
Job 39

WEEK 4

Amazing Grace

———•◆•———

19

Grace recalled

Just before leaving for church, we received a phone call from the hospital. The birth of our first grandchild was imminent. Much excited we told the congregation on arrival that for once we were deliberately going to leave our mobile phone on. Then we heard nothing. The ministry of the word complete, we shared the Peace and I announced the third hymn, 'Amazing grace'. Preoccupied with singing this great hymn while preparing for communion, I never noticed my wife slipping outside the church to answer the phone.

It was a moment few in the congregation will ever forget. As we completed the final words of 'Amazing grace' – 'We've no less days to sing God's praise/Than when we've first begun' – my wife rushed back in shouting, 'It's a boy – William!'

'Amazing grace' has an unusual history of its own. It also has much to say about a Christian understanding of grace and will form the theme this week.

First published in the collection known as the *Olney Hymns* in 1779, its author, John Newton, was at the time the Anglican priest in charge of Olney. The following year he became rector of St Mary Woolnoth in the City of London and remained there until his death in 1807.

Quite a number of the *Olney Hymns* – such as 'Glorious things of thee are spoken' and 'How sweet the name of Jesus sounds' – were quickly established as favourites both in the Church of England and in the Free Churches. However 'Amazing grace' took rather longer to find a place in British hymnbooks. It was not included in the Anglican *Hymns Ancient and Modern* or *The English Hymnal*, nor was it included in the traditional hymnbooks of Presbyterians, Methodists or Baptists.

This is curious. It has long been a favourite hymn at weddings and funerals. Indeed, anyone attending a wedding in Scotland is likely to hear its familiar tune blasted out on the bagpipes as the newly married couple leaves the kirk. And it frequently appears among the top ten favourite hymns in opinion polls. Yet, until the publication of *Mission Praise*[2], many congregations had to photocopy it for use in a service.

Its earlier popularity in Britain owed much to the Sunday-school movement. It was one of the English hymns reimported from America through the influence of Moody and Sankey before the First World War. The words are by an Englishman, but its catchy tune is based upon a traditional American melody. And it was in America that it first became popular. In Britain it has remained in the memories of many older people who once went to Sunday school. It represents a powerful memory of childhood faith. Of grace recalled.

The other curious feature of this popular hymn is its author. When John Newton died at the age of 82, the epitaph on his memorial (composed by himself) read as follows:

JOHN NEWTON CLERK
ONCE AN INFIDEL AND LIBERTINE
A SERVANT OF SLAVES IN AFRICA
WAS BY THE RICH MERCY OF OUR LORD
AND SAVIOUR

JESUS CHRIST
PRESERVED, RESTORED AND PARDONED
AND APPOINTED TO PREACH THE FAITH
HE HAD LONG LABOURED TO DESTROY

The author of this influential hymn about God's grace had a most unusual background for a priest and hymn writer – he had once been a slave-trader. This epitaph, which can still be seen in St Mary Woolnoth, was intended to shock.

John Newton saw himself, in line with St Paul, as one who had once deliberately tried to destroy the faith but had been dramatically converted by God's grace. He wrote and preached extensively about this conversion and about the horrors of his young life. And he often used this experience, mixed with biblical allusions, in his popular hymns (this week several meditations will be drawn from biblical passages that were particularly important to him – starting with 1 Chronicles 17.16–17 which shaped 'Amazing grace').

His hymns take on a new meaning when they are placed side by side with the story of his extraordinary life. This is 'Amazing grace' as it appeared in Ira D. Sankey's original *Sacred Songs and Solos*:

Amazing grace, how sweet the sound,
That saved a wretch like me!
I once was lost, but now am found;
Was blind, but now I see.

'Twas grace that taught my heart to fear,
And grace my fears relieved;
How precious did that grace appear,
The hour I first believed.

Through many dangers, toils and snares,
I have already come;
'Tis grace that brought me safe thus far,

And grace will lead me home.

Yes, when this heart and flesh shall fail,
And mortal life shall cease,
I shall possess, within the vail,
A life of joy and peace.

Most modern versions of this hymn stay with the basic words of the first three verses, but some versions include a further verse before the final one:

The Lord has promised good to me,
His words my hope secures;
My shield and stronghold he shall be
As long as life endures.

Mission Praise keeps to four verses, but radically changes the last one:

When we've been there ten thousand years
Bright shining as the sun,
We've no less days to sing God's praise
Than when we've first begun.

The words of 'Amazing grace' are still changing more than 200 years after John Newton's death.

MEDITATION
1 Chronicles 17.16–17

20

Childhood grace

The first verse of 'Amazing grace' has a stark contrast:

I once was lost, but now am found;
Was blind, but now I see.

In all probability it was not as simple as this in real life.
Perhaps it never is.

In his autobiography, written when he was 39 years old and
just about to be ordained, John Newton remembered his
childhood more accurately:

How far the best education may fall short of reaching the
heart will strongly appear in the sequel of my history: yet I
think, for the encouragement of pious parents to go on in
the good way of doing their part faithfully to form their
children's minds, I may properly propose myself as an
instance. Though in process of time I sinned away all the
advantages of these early impressions, yet they were for a
great while a restraint upon me; they returned again and
again, and it was very long before I could wholly shake
them off; and when the Lord at length opened my eyes, I
found great benefit from the recollection of them.[3]

His mother died when he was only seven, but he could still
remember her as a pious chapel-goer. Soon after, his father, a
shipmaster, remarried and this clearly caused the young child
many problems. Yet, in several places in the autobiography,
his father appears to have been genuinely concerned about his
son's moral welfare. And, as a teenager, John did at times

practise his faith. He even recalled that 'sometimes when I had determined on things, which I knew were sinful and contrary to my duty, I could not go on quietly, till I had first despatched my ordinary task of prayer'. He even fasted and read the Bible at great length. However, like St Augustine of Hippo in the fourth century, his problem as a young man in the eighteenth century was that 'I often saw the necessity of religion . . . but I loved sin, and was unwilling to forsake it'[4].

It is only too natural. In order to persuade others about the truth of the Christian faith, it is tempting to portray youthful conversion as a complete about-turn. Again and again in his autobiography and letters, John Newton used 'blindness' as a negative image (as John Hull might note). Before his conversion he was totally 'blind and stupid', whereas after his conversion he could 'see'.

Interviewers of the extraordinary modern composer, John Tavener, often mention his 'conversion' to Greek Orthodoxy when he was in his thirties. His life before his conversion is usually portrayed as worldly and somewhat dissolute. Following conversion his life has been dedicated, instead, to sacred music – music that has become famous around the world as a result of Princess Diana's funeral.

Occasionally interviewers also note that he was a church organist for many years before he converted to Greek Orthodoxy. By an odd fluke we were at school together. I can remember a conversation that we had when we were both eight (I am sure he has long forgotten it). Neither of us could play cricket, so we were left to chat at deep field. To our surprise we discovered that we had both concluded that nothing was more important in life than religious faith, and that we were both amazed that our other friends could not see this. I remain amazed and, I guess, John Tavener does too. Without being especially pious, some people find religious faith simply inescapable.

My guess is that John Newton was similar, but of course he

was brought up at a time (unlike today) when almost everyone would have had some acquaintance with the church.

One of the most crucial factors is childhood. Studies of adult 'converts' and of adults who start going to church, show that they have usually been exposed to religious faith as children. There are occasional examples of adults, with absolutely no previous connection with religious faith, suddenly becoming practising Christians. Yet it is much more usual for adults to return to a faith that they once knew in childhood or youth. Of course some never return. There is nothing inevitable about this. Yet it is distinctly less likely that someone with no religious background whatsoever will ever become a practising Christian.

At a time when the proportion of young people in church or Sunday school in Britain is lower than it has been for at least 150 years, this is a worrying finding. There should be considerable concern in churches about whether many youngsters today (with little or no acquaintance with organized Christianity) will ever become practising Christians in later life. But that is another story.

What John Newton's autobiography suggests is that the child was not too unlike the man. It was perhaps never quite the case, as he claimed, that he 'sinned away all the advantages' of his Christian upbringing. His wild years at sea did seem for a while to overshadow this upbringing. Yet grace in childhood was later recalled.

MEDITATION
Luke 13.18–21

21

Fall from grace

John Newton was first taken to sea as a teenager by his merchant seaman father. However, as a young man he was captured by a press-gang and, following the brutal practice of the time, was impressed against his will into naval service. As a result he became a midshipman on a man-of-war fighting against the Dutch in the 1740s.

Very much against his father's wishes, he fell in love with Mary Cutlett, whose family lived near Maidstone in Kent. They were not to get married until 1750, so for some years he visited her in secret. Unfortunately this got him into serious trouble with the navy (as well as with his father). Having received permission to go ashore briefly, on one occasion he took the opportunity to visit Mary Cutlett instead. When he returned a day late, he was flogged and demoted for attempting to desert.

His father was appalled. Perhaps to cool his relationship with Mary Cutlett (as many other fathers have vainly attempted to do), or perhaps simply to extricate him from the navy, he arranged for his son to be transferred back into a merchant ship. However, this time it was a slave-trading ship heading for the west coast of Africa. For the next decade he was employed in this appalling trade.

In his autobiography John Newton recalled the sinful life he led while working as a slave-trader. To a modern reader it is extraordinary that it was his personal life as a youth that concerned him rather than his work in the slave-trade. Like many other sailors, he drank too much, swore and womanized. Yet it was only many years later, under the influence of William Wilberforce, that he campaigned against the slave-trade itself.

In common with others at the time, he probably regarded trading slaves as morally acceptable. After all, many of the slave owners in the West Indies, importing slaves in vast numbers with horrendous suffering from West Africa, were themselves practising Christians. Even some of the missionary bodies in Barbados owned slaves. And, for six years after his dramatic conversion, John Newton himself continued to work in the slave-trade. It was private, rather than public, morality that caused John Newton such agonies of guilt.

For a while after his conversion, he reported that 'I concluded, at first, that my sins were too great to be forgiven'. He was particularly concerned about 'the licentious courses of my conversation'[5]. He had regularly blasphemed. On one occasion he became so helplessly drunk that he nearly dived over board when he had no idea how to swim. Fortunately, his friends grabbed his feet just as he was about to disappear. And in African ports there were numerous opportunities to sleep with the local women (his autobiography only hints at this . . . it is a discrete document written for a Christian audience). Yet it was his blasphemies that troubled him most once he became a believing Christian again.

So, even his fall from grace took a distinctly religious turn. As his epitaph stated so clearly, he believed that his final downfall as a young man was that 'he had long laboured to destroy' the Christian faith. Of course he had also been a 'libertine' and 'a servant of slaves in Africa' [no mention of being a slave-trader]. Yet blaspheming was far worse in his eyes.

One of the most disturbing thoughts is to wonder what it will be about twenty-first-century Christians that twenty-fourth-century Christians will find most shocking. Will it be that we failed to denounce clearly the evils of the arms trade? Or that we tolerated poverty and hunger in the world? Or that we were half-hearted in our concerns about ecology and the environment? Or what? Sometimes we imagine that as Christians we can have a clear-sighted understanding of moral evil. Yet our track record suggests that it is at best partial-sight.

Whatever his own limitations as an eighteenth-century person, when he was in his mid-twenties John Newton came to believe that his personal life was in a mess. He did not believe anything, he was existing simply for passing pleasures, and he was deeply conscious that he was not living up to his dead mother's pious hopes for him. He was also spending most of his life at sea and in Africa, while his beloved Mary Cutlett was at home in Kent. In short, his personal life had become deeply fragile.

This is quite common for those who experience a radical religious conversion. Ahead of such a conversion there is often quite a long period of increasing fragility. For St Augustine of Hippo, and perhaps for St Paul as well, this experience of fragility stretched over many years. Although the conversion itself can appear as just a single moment, it is often preceded by such experience. Life appears to become shallow and pointless. Pleasures, once pursued with great vigour, become vacuous and even painful. There is a growing sense that there must be more to life than this . . . a sense of meaning and purpose reaching beyond a trivial life.

John Newton was at last ready for a sense of grace.

———◆———

MEDITATION
Luke 13.6–9

22

Grace rediscovered

On 21 March 1748 John Newton's life changed radically. He was 23 years old. The slave-ship he worked on was caught in a violent Atlantic storm and nearly sank. In his autobiography, written 16 years later, he recalled the exact moment of change:

> About nine o'clock, being almost spent with cold and labour, I went to speak to the captain, who was busied elsewhere, and just as I was returning from him, I said, almost without meaning: 'If this will not do, the Lord have mercy upon us.' This (though spoken with little reflection), was the first desire I had breathed for mercy for the space of many years.[6]

Later, John Newton was to see this as a defining moment in his life, parallel to Jesus' parable of the prodigal son (Luke 15.11–32). After all, the son in this parable had rejected everything his father stood for. He, too, had gone abroad and 'squandered his property in loose living' and sleeping with prostitutes. Then, faced with a life-threatening emergency, he had returned home with the plea: 'Father, I have sinned against heaven and before you; I am no longer worthy to be called your son.' John Newton saw this as a clear example of 'the Lord's goodness to returning sinners'[7] and was convinced that it closely fitted his own life as a young man.

At the time his analysis was less clear-cut:

> I continued at the pump from three in the morning till near noon, and then I could do no more: I went and lay down

upon my bed, uncertain and almost indifferent whether I should ever rise again. In an hour's time I was called, and not being able to pump, I went to the helm and steered the ship till midnight, excepting a small interval for refreshment. I had leisure and convenient opportunity for reflection: I began to think of my former religious professions; the extraordinary turns in my life; the calls, warnings, and deliverances I had met with . . . I waited with fear and impatience to receive my inevitable doom.[8]

As we know, he did survive the storm. The badly damaged ship managed, with considerable difficulty, to struggle back to port.

However, in his own mind, John Newton had reached a sharp turning-point in his life. He had made the plea 'the Lord have mercy upon us' and the ship and crew had survived. Even so, it still took him several years to understand this dramatic experience in terms of grace:

Yet, though I had thoughts of this kind, they were exceedingly faint and disproportionate; it was not till long after (perhaps several years), when I gained some clear views of the infinite righteousness and grace of Christ Jesus, my Lord, that I had a deep and strong apprehension of my state by nature and practice, and, perhaps, till then I could not have borne the sight. So wonderfully does the Lord proportion the discoveries of sin and grace.[9]

He was to spend the rest of his life telling this story over and over again. Rekindling this initial sense of grace:

'Twas grace that taught my heart to fear,
And grace my fears relieved;
How precious did that grace appear,
The hour I first believed.

Nevertheless, there was a puzzle. The near disaster of the storm had deeply affected him. He had faced the likelihood of imminent death, but somehow had been spared:

> Through many dangers, toils and snares,
> I have already come;
> 'Tis grace that brought me safe thus far,
> And grace will lead me home.

Yet, when he talked to the other sailors who had also survived, he found that they had apparently been left quite unmoved. As he wrote in his autobiography:

> My companions in danger were either quite unaffected, or soon forgot it all, but it was not so with me: but because the Lord was pleased to vouchsafe me peculiar mercy, otherwise I was the most unlikely person to receive an impression, having been often before quite stupid and hardened in the very face of great dangers.[10]

He eventually came to see this as a special sign of grace. The Lord had chosen him – the very one who had tried to destroy the Christian faith – to experience this strong sense of grace. It was not his own goodness that was responsible for this sense of grace. Rather the opposite. He regarded himself as the sinner and feared that 'my sins were too great to be forgiven'. It was God's mercy alone that was responsible for this sense of grace. John Newton, the sinner, had been chosen by God. This remained his firm conviction driving his later ministry as an Anglican priest.

Yet the puzzle remains. A dramatic moment is shared by two people. One sees it as just a dramatic moment, whereas the other sees it as a signal of grace, as evidence of God's help in his or her life.

Or there is some shared moment of exquisite beauty or tenderness. Again for one person it remains just that and nothing more. Whereas for another, such a moment evokes, in addition, a sense of grace.

MEDITATION
Luke 15.11–32

23

Poets of grace

In 1764 John Newton was ordained, becoming the curate in charge of the parish priest at Olney. Three years later the poet William Cowper moved into the same parish. Then for the next six years they had a remarkable partnership, writing hymns in order to share their faith with the parishioners.

William Cowper was six years younger than John Newton. His father was rector of Great Berkhamsted, but he himself trained as a lawyer. Sadly, as a young man he began to suffer from serious attacks of depression and became suicidal. He gave up law and went instead to live with his brother (also an Anglican priest) and sister-in-law. It was when his brother died that he came, with his sister-in-law, to Olney. However after six fruitful years his depression and suicidal feelings returned and John Newton had to take most of the responsibility for publishing their joint collection of *Olney Hymns* in 1779.

The two men shared a very similar faith. Both had known deep experiences of a sense of grace and both also knew bleaker moments. In fact, it was when his depression and suicidal feelings were starting again that William Cowper wrote one his most enduring hymns:

> God moves in a mysterious way,
> His wonders to perform;
> He plants his footsteps in the sea,
> And rides upon the storm.
>
> Deep in unfathomable mines
> Of never-failing skill

He treasures up his bright designs,
And works his sovereign will.

Together with the final verse, it is one of the finest hymns reflecting a Job-like sense of the great mystery of God:

Blind unbelief is sure to err,
And scan his work in vain;
God is his own interpreter,
And he will make it plain.

However, it is two of the middle verses that reflect the sense of personal fragility, coupled with a sense of God's grace, that the two hymn writers shared:

Ye faithful saints, fresh courage take;
The clouds ye so much dread
Are big with mercy, and shall break
In blessings on your head.

Judge not the Lord by feeble sense,
But trust him for his grace;
Behind a frowning providence
He hides a smiling face.

This double sense of fragility and grace is again strongly present in William Cowper's haunting, but painful, hymn 'Hark, my soul! It is the Lord'. In two middle verses he imagines Jesus saying to his soul:

I delivered thee when bound,
And when bleeding, healed thy wound;
Sought thee wandering, set thee right;
Turned thy darkness into light.

Can a woman's tender care
Cease towards the child she bare?

Yes, she may forgetful be,
Yet will I remember thee.

Note the unexpected, and troubled, 'yes' in that last verse.
And, then, in the final verse William Cowper longs for grace
beyond his fragility:

Lord, it is my chief complaint
That my love is weak and faint;
Yet I love thee, and adore;
O for grace to love thee more!

A very similar longing for grace (for God's help) beyond personal fragility is found in the first three verses of John
Newton's hymn, also included in *Olney Hymns*:

How sweet the name of Jesus sounds
In a believer's ear!
It soothes his sorrows, heals his wounds,
And drives away his fear.

It makes the wounded spirit whole,
And calms the troubled breast;
'Tis manna to the hungry soul,
And to the weary rest.

Dear name! The rock on which I build,
My shield and hiding place,
My never-failing treasury, filled
With boundless stores of grace.

John Newton believed passionately that hymns offered a
means to share Christian faith with non-churchgoers, to evoke
in otherwise secular people a sense of grace. He persuaded his
friend William Cowper to use his superior poetic talents to do
the same. The hymns that resulted were then circulated widely

in the Olney area long before they were actually published. John Newton encouraged people to sing them in churches and chapels (he was instrumental in bringing churches and chapels in Olney together at a time of sharp rivalry between denominations), as well as in the open air and at home. In this way he hoped that these hymns might shape the lives of those who sang and heard them.

Of course John Newton and William Cowper were not alone. John and Charles Wesley were at this very time using hymns as an essential part of popular Methodism. And a generation earlier than all four of these hymn writers, the Congregationalist Isaac Watts had pioneered congregational hymn singing, writing such enduring hymns as 'Jesus shall reign where'er the sun' and 'When I survey the wondrous cross'.

Through these gifted writers, people in the eighteenth century began to discover the power of hymn singing as a means of bringing dreary Anglican worship to life. A means of evoking a sense of grace.

———•◆•———

MEDITATION
Acts 2.43–47

24

If I, through grace, a member am

Becoming rector of St Mary Woolnoth in the City of London
in 1780 was a very significant promotion for John Newton.
He was determined to use the opportunity to encourage others to take the Christian faith seriously. At Olney he had written his hymns to do this, now he could use a famous London
pulpit as well. Whereas quite a number of incumbents in the
City of London had been appointed by their rich relatives, he
had been promoted rather for his zeal, energy and faith.

His correspondence at the time shows the many connections
he made while at St Mary Woolnoth. This was a man still
driven by the dramatic experience of a sense of grace he had
when he was 23. Every year he gave thanks in his diary on the
anniversary of his conversion.

Then in 1790 Mary Cutlett, the girl he had finally married
40 years earlier, died. William Cowper wrote an affectionate,
but typically ironic, letter to him a month after her death:

> My dear Friend, – Had you been a man of the world, I
> should have held myself bound by the law of ceremonies to
> have sent you long since my tribute of condolence. I have
> sincerely mourned with you; and though you have lost a
> wife, and I only a friend, yet do I understand too well the
> value of such a friend as Mrs Newton not to have sympa-
> thized with you very nearly. But you are not a man of this
> world; neither can you, who have both the Scripture and
> the Giver of Scripture to console you, have any need of aid
> from others, or expect it from such spiritual imbecility as
> mine.[11]

A Sense of Grace

After all the years of deep depression and 'madness' (he was placed in an asylum on more than one occasion), William Cowper had clearly lost none of his wit or skill with words. As one Christian corresponding as a friend with another, he knew that he was not writing to 'a man of this world', or to one who would have considered death (however painful at the moment) to be tragic extinction. He would also have been very familiar with the final verse of one of John Newton's most famous hymns, 'Glorious things of thee are spoken':

Saviour, if of Zion's city
I, through grace, a member am,
Let the world deride or pity,
I will glory in thy name.
Fading is the worldling's pleasure,
All his boasted pomp and show;
Solid joys and lasting treasure
None but Zion's children know.

What both men believed was that the 'solid joys' of a sense of grace far outweighed any worldly pleasures. They also outweighed the moments of depression that both men experienced. William Cowper experienced very severe mood swings between deep depression and a sense of grace. There appeared to be a touch of the manic-depressive about John Newton as well. His hymns suggest this, as does his correspondence. Some of the most significant Christian thinkers in history may have had similar mood swings – including, perhaps, St Paul, St Augustine and Martin Luther. Like many other creative writers, composers and artists, these mood swings may even have helped them to have insights about experience that the rest of us know only in part. The very intensity of their experience helps us to see similar, but less intense, aspects of our own experience.

John Newton was now 65, but he lived another 17 years, refusing all the time to consider retirement. A year before his death, his friends tried hard to persuade him otherwise – mentioning, significantly, his continuing moments of depression:

> They marked not only his infirmities in the pulpit, but felt much account of the decrease of his strength and his occasional depressions . . . 'I cannot stop!' said he, raising his voice. 'What! Shall the old African blasphemer stop while he can speak?'[12]

John Newton (unlike poor William Cowper) had learned to live with depression. Instead, a strong sense of grace sustained him to the very end. Whatever his physical or mental frailties, he was determined to remain rector of St Mary Woolnoth until he died.

If, in his autobiography, he saw his life mirrored in Jesus' parable of the prodigal son, he also found it depicted in the opening chapter of the first letter to Timothy. These verses are especially poignant:

> I am grateful to Christ Jesus our Lord, who has strengthened me, because he judged me faithful and appointed me to his service, even though I was formerly a blasphemer, a persecutor, and a man of violence. But I received mercy because I had acted ignorantly in unbelief, and the grace of our Lord overflowed for me with the faith and love that are in Christ Jesus. (1 Timothy 1.12–14)

MEDITATION
1 Timothy 1.12–17

WEEK 5

Shaped by Grace

25

Grace through weakness

At the very beginning of this book, I told the story of my grandfather, as a young curate, trying hard not to laugh when he preached on the text, 'My grace is sufficient for you' (2 Corinthians 12.9). His problem was not with the text itself but with the way it had been playfully changed by a fellow curate.

Having unravelled some of the different meanings of 'grace' in previous weeks – some more Christian than others – it is time in Week 5 to return to this great text, looking at its wider context in the second letter of St Paul to the Corinthians. And if Week 4 explored grace in the extraordinary life of John Newton, Week 5, instead, explores grace in more ordinary lives.

One of the ironies about Paul in his various letters is that he is often at his most lyrical when doing battle with opponents. For example, he gives us the earliest account of the institution of the Lord's Supper (1 Corinthians 11.23–26) immediately after scolding the Corinthian Christians for their quarrelling, drunkenness and greed when sharing the Lord's Supper together. Again, set in the middle of references to the bad behaviour of some Christians,

Paul gives us the lyrical words of what is sometimes termed the Philippian hymn (Philippians 2.6–11).

2 Corinthians 12 is no exception. In the previous chapter Paul talks about 'false apostles' and 'deceitful workers'. To rebut them he engages in a litany of 'boasting', knowing that in doing so 'I am speaking as a fool'. He recounts at length the sufferings and persecutions he has endured within his Christian ministry: imprisonments, floggings, shipwrecks, a stoning, physical hardships, hunger, cold:

> Who is weak, and I am not weak? Who is made to stumble, and I am not indignant? If I must boast, I will boast of the things that show my weakness. The God and Father of the Lord Jesus (blessed be he for ever!) knows that I do not lie. (2 Corinthians 11.29–31)

The connection between all of this and 'grace' is made earlier in this letter in chapter 4. There Paul insists that the very weakness of the early followers of Christ is evidence that the new power they receive is not their own power but God's. To make this point he takes the everyday Mediterranean image of treasure kept in a humble clay jar:

> But we have this treasure in clay jars, so that it may be made clear that this extraordinary power belongs to God and does not come from us. We are afflicted in every way, but not crushed; perplexed, but not driven to despair; persecuted, but not forsaken; struck down, but not destroyed; always carrying in the body the death of Jesus, so that the life of Jesus may also be made visible in our bodies. (2 Corinthians 4.7–10)

There is a theme of reverse images running through many early Christian writings. The world at large envies political power, intellectual power, wealth and prestige. These are the signs of true status for many people, past and present. However, this is all reversed for a true follower of Christ. Paul frequently contrasts his own 'foolishness' with the sort of wisdom that is so much admired by the world. Wealth and prestige can no longer be goals of the Christian. All of this is starkly reversed in Christ.

However the point about 'grace' that Paul makes in 2 Corinthians goes beyond this reversal. It is not simply that Christ reverses the signs of status taken so seriously by the world at large. It is also that the power of God working through those who are now in Christ is shown through our very weakness. The good that we do is manifestly not ours, since we are so obviously weak. Rather it can clearly be seen to be the grace of God working in and through us – evidence, indeed, that God is helping us in our lives.

That is why he can later 'boast' about all the suffering and persecution he has had to endure in his Christian ministry. For Paul suffering and persecution are not occasions for personal pride or satisfaction. Emphatically, he is not claiming (as critics have sometimes insisted) that he actually enjoys this suffering and persecution.

Instead, what he is saying to the Corinthian Christians (and now to us) is that anyone looking at Christian behaviour should be able to see the hand of God at work . . . not because Christians are wonderful, but because, left to our own devices, we are so obviously weak. The good that we do cannot possibly be our good. It must be God's good at work through us.

Having reached this conclusion, Paul then argues that grace should be spread in the world in and through us: 'Yes, everything is for your sake, so that grace, as it extends to more and more people, may increase thanksgiving, to the glory of God' (2 Corinthians 4.15).

Grace shining through weakness.

MEDITATION
2 Corinthians 4.1–15

26

Persecuted grace

One of the most moving moments in my life was meeting people in China who had personally experienced anti-religious persecution. First in Beijing and then in Xian I met several people of my own age, all brought up in religious families, who had experienced at first hand the horrors of the Cultural Revolution 40 years earlier.

There was a Buddhist abbot. Speaking through an interpreter, he welcomed me to take tea in his office at the heart of a busy Buddhist temple. Largely off the tourist route, this is a working temple and monastery, training young men to be monks and serving the wider population. At festivals thousands of local people crowd into the temple grounds. The abbot told me that the Chinese government was now encouraging such temples – seeing them as a force for good citizenship – and even providing grants for them to restore buildings that had been damaged during the Cultural Revolution.

For him this represented a huge change. Generations of his family had become Buddhist monks and were deeply committed to the protection and study of Buddhist scripture. However, as the Cultural Revolution took hold across China, his family warned him that their scriptures would soon be destroyed and that it was his duty to commit them entirely to memory. This he did. The sacred books were indeed destroyed, but the sacred ideas within them survived in his head. Then, when eventually the political situation changed, he wrote them down on paper once more. Today, all around the ornate temple and monastery, young men can be seen sitting cross-legged, studying and reciting these restored Buddhist scriptures.

The abbot was fascinated to hear about churches in Britain.

He especially wanted to know what we 'did' about religious sects. Still regarded as a threat to stability within modern China, they are not tolerated or supported in the way that mainstream Buddhist, Christian or Muslim temples, churches and mosques increasingly are. Some persecution remains, as well as strong memories of persecution, and the state is still officially atheist, so caution is needed. Yet for the moment, at least, he reported that Buddhist practice was now both permitted and spreading fast.

A Catholic priest spoke excellent English and could report more directly. He, too, remembered life as a boy during the Cultural Revolution. No longer able to go to mass, his family said prayers and read the Bible privately, while carefully warning the children not to mention their faith to anybody else. This was purely a family devotion. Just one Catholic church – the Southern Cathedral in Beijing – remained open during the Cultural Revolution. However it was only open to foreigners, not to the Chinese people themselves. Then gradually restrictions began to be eased and Catholic churches, once used for secular purposes, were restored one by one for worship. As he showed me the great Northern Cathedral in Beijing, he recalled how his whole family had been in tears when first allowed to attend mass again there. After all the years of private devotion, at last they could be public Christians again.

In Xian a Protestant, middle-aged layworker had a similar story to tell. As she proudly showed me her church, a plain building bursting with chairs and crowded at every service, she too remembered the time when her family was forced to pray in secret. It was a dangerous time then to be identified in public as a Christian. She spoke excitedly about the new religious freedom in Xian and encouraged me to go to the Great Mosque to see that this applied to Muslims as much as to Christians.

Most fascinating of all was to meet a group of six young Catholics in the Southern Cathedral. All without brothers and sisters (following government policy), each had found a very individual path to becoming a Christian. One had listened to Gospel singing broadcasts from Hong Kong for several years before actually going to church. Another had made connections through literature, noticing, for example, references to Noah's ark in a novel. Some explained that giving Christmas cards was still popular in Beijing, even after the Cultural Revolution. This allowed churches to make connections between the secular snow scenes they depicted and the baby at Bethlehem. Several reported that it was at the midnight mass at the Southern Cathedral that they had first been excited by Christian worship.

Despite the Cultural Revolution, Christian memories remained among some in China. Within a number of families, memories were sustained by family prayer. Among others they were carried less directly within cultural symbols, such as the Christmas cards. In one church hall two huge posters stood waiting to be put outside the church entrance next Christmas. The one on the left was a picture of Santa Claus, whereas the one on the right was a blue-eyed, blond-haired Jesus. Placed together their public message was clear: 'You all know who the one on the left is. Well, the one on the right goes with him!'

Grace surviving persecution.

MEDITATION
2 Corinthians 4.16—5.3

27

Generous grace

I remember going as a schoolboy to hear John Collins, the radical canon at St Paul's Cathedral, talking at Westminster Hall to a meeting of Christians opposing nuclear weapons. Halfway through the meeting he announced he was going to appeal for money for the cause. He warned us that we were all going to get overexcited and would end up giving much more generously than we might have expected. An expert at whipping up crowds, he then proceeded to do exactly that. I gave every penny in my pockets and, instead of catching a bus, had to walk for my train home.

I suspect that Paul had the same skill. Encouraging people to generous giving. Generous grace is an important theme in Paul. As already seen, he insists that grace should be spread in the world in and through us: 'Yes, everything is for your sake, so that grace, as it extends to more and more people, may increase thanksgiving, to the glory of God' (2 Corinthians 4.15).

This is a bold claim and it gets bolder. Paul next compares life with or without faith to life in a house or in a tent:

> For we know that if the earthly tent we live in is destroyed, we have a building from God, a house not made with hands, eternal in the heavens. For in this tent we groan, longing to be clothed with our heavenly dwelling. (2 Corinthians 5.1–2)

Scholars are divided on whether Paul is talking about a life of faith here and now, or life beyond death. The same ambiguity is often present in the Gospels when Jesus talks about the kingdom of God – it does seem to be both present and future.

Perhaps, life in Christ, known partly now, but with a hope of greater glory later.

Certainly there is a tension running throughout Paul's letter between the Christian life as it ought to be and the more messy lives that the Corinthian Christians are actually leading. Little has changed today.

Paul becomes lyrical when depicting this life as it ought to be:

> So if anyone is in Christ, there is a new creation: everything old has passed away; see, everything has become new! All this is from God, who reconciled us to himself through Christ, and has given us the ministry of reconciliation; that is, in Christ God was reconciling the world to himself, not counting their trespasses against them, and entrusting the message of reconciliation to us. So we are ambassadors for Christ, since God is making his appeal through us. (2 Corinthians 5.17–20)

Then, immediately, he adds: 'we entreat you on behalf of Christ, be reconciled to God'. So, clearly there is a gap – a gap between the demands of grace and the actuality of grace in frail human lives. This gap becomes obvious in the very next verse: 'As we work together with him, we urge you also not to accept the grace of God in vain' (2 Corinthians 6.1).

Some scholars see these sharp swings of tone as evidence that 2 Corinthians has been pieced together from several of Paul's letters to the young church in Corinth. Others disagree and see the letter as a single whole. It probably does not matter very much. Whether Paul was writing in different moods on different occasions, or had swings of mood while writing a single letter, he was manifestly struggling with a tension that is at the very heart of Christian life. It is simply this: There is always a gap between life in Christ as it ought to be and that life as it actually is. If we are honest with ourselves, all church-goers will be only too conscious of this gap.

The gap remains in the chapters that follow. In chapter 7 Paul talks frankly about the grief experienced earlier by the Corinthian Christians when he had to scold them. Because of their new-found earnestness, he does not regret doing this, painful as undoubtedly it was at the time.

Then in the next chapter, he talks about generous giving – simultaneously praising the generosity of some and urging others to follow:

> We want you to know, brothers and sisters, about the grace of God that has been granted to the churches of Macedonia; for during a severe ordeal of affliction, their abundant joy and their extreme poverty have overflowed in a wealth of generosity on their part. For, as I can testify, they voluntarily gave according to their means, and even beyond their means . . . Now as you excel in everything – in faith, in speech, in knowledge, in utmost eagerness, and in our love for you – so we want you to excel also in this generous undertaking. (2 Corinthians 8.1–3 and 7)

Note that final sentence. Having told the Corinthian Christians about the wonderful generosity of the impoverished churches of Macedonia, Paul immediately launches into an appeal for them to match this generosity themselves.

Paul still speaks to us.

MEDITATION
2 Corinthians 8.1–15

28

Measuring grace

I spent several years on a research project analysing the results of scores of opinion polls. At the time there was considerable debate about whether or not churchgoing had any effect upon people's values and behaviour. Opinion polls undoubtedly have their limitations, but I wanted to see whether, used cautiously, they could detect any differences between churchgoers and non-churchgoers.

When first told that I was planning to do this research, university colleagues were sceptical. Some said it was unlikely that any real differences of value or behaviour would be found between churchgoers and non-churchgoers. For many of them churchgoing is a marginal activity having little or no effect upon those going to church. Another group of my colleagues was quite scathing. They claimed that churchgoers are different from other people – they are more racist and pro-capital punishment. My results, they predicted, would confirm this.

Cheered on by their 'encouragement', I decided I did want to know the truth, whatever the results. In the event, these results were more positive than any of us had expected.

Specifically Christian beliefs – for example, beliefs in a personal God, in the divinity of Christ, or in a life beyond this one – were much higher among churchgoers than non-churchgoers. These beliefs certainly did not disappear among non-churchgoers (especially if they went to church as children), but they were much weaker. Among those going to church every week they were strongest of all. Poll after poll showed that Christian beliefs were still held by a sizeable proportion of the British population. However, the more regularly individuals went to church, the stronger were their beliefs.

This finding was hardly surprising. What was more surprising was the finding that similar differences could be detected on moral values and behaviour. Churchgoers shared values and patterns of behaviour with a wide section of society. Yet these values and patterns of behaviour were found more strongly among churchgoers and were weakest among those who never went to church.

Questions about personal honesty showed this clearly. Those interviewed in some polls were told about some common situation – for example, being given too much change at a supermarket checkout – and were asked about how they would respond. Churchgoers were more likely than others to say they would act honestly and return the change. Or they were asked about whether or not they had ever written to their MP about some local injustice. Or again, they were asked about the value of faithfulness within a marriage. In response to a range of similar questions, it appeared that virtues such as honesty were valued by a wide section of the public, yet they were valued more highly still by churchgoers.

One of the sharpest differences was on charitable giving. Non-churchgoers were distinctly more inclined than churchgoers to believe that 'charity begins at home'. Churchgoers were much more likely to believe that the poor overseas should also receive financial help from British charities. In addition, levels of charitable giving did seem to be particularly high among the most committed churchgoers.

Another distinct difference was on voluntary work in the community. Someone who goes regularly to church is some two or three times more likely to be actively engaged in secular, voluntary work than someone who seldom or never goes to church. Of course it is essential to balance this finding. Those who go regularly to church tend to be older than those who do not, and there are more women than men among them. Older women tend to be more active than others in the wider community. Yet this finding still holds true for younger men who go regularly to church. In fact, many charities would be severely stretched if they lost all of their churchgoing volunteers. Even those that see themselves as secular charities – such as Oxfam or Shelter – would be stretched.

So perhaps Paul was right after all. There really does seem to be evidence that the churches at Macedonia have their counterparts in Britain today – and that churchgoing shapes people to be genuine ambassadors of Christ in the community.

There may be another explanation for this, as my university colleagues would be quick to point out. It could be that people who already hold these values are attracted to churchgoing, rather than that churchgoing shapes their values. To test this possibility I looked carefully at two groups of non-churchgoers. One group had been to church regularly as children, and the other not. Interestingly some of the differences between churchgoers and non-churchgoers were also detected between these two groups as well. This does suggest that even involuntary churchgoing as a child has a lasting effect upon someone's values and behaviour. So it does seem that churches, not only attract people with certain values, but also shape them as well.

Yet the gap between values and action already seen in Paul is also present in the opinion poll evidence. Churchgoers are more inclined than others to be honest, faithful and volunteering in the community than others. Yet some churchgoers appear not to be. And there are many non-churchgoers who do appear to be. These are, at most, relative differences. Although churchgoers turn out to be better than my sceptical colleagues had predicted (they are also less racist and pro-capital punishment than others), they are only relatively better than other people.

There are still plenty of Christians living in tents.

———— ◆ ————

MEDITATION
2 Corinthians 9.1–15

29

Sufficient grace

It is time to put the text 'My grace is sufficient for you' properly into context. As we have seen, Paul has already argued, in his letter to the Corinthians, that a sense of grace (a sense that God is helping us in our lives) becomes most apparent within human weakness. Grace is the treasure – manifestly coming from God – to be found in the clay jars of frail human beings attempting to follow Christ. Grace – if only we will accept it – can enable us to be ambassadors of Christ in the world.

Now Paul adds another dimension altogether. He recalls an extraordinary mystical vision and moment of personal revelation. Famously, he recalls it using the third person, almost as if he wants to hide the fact that it is obviously his own experience he is writing about:

> I know a person in Christ who fourteen years ago was caught up to the third heaven – whether in the body or out of the body I do not know; God knows. And I know that such a person – whether in the body or out of the body I do not know; God knows – was caught up into Paradise and heard things that are not to be told, that no mortal is permitted to repeat. (2 Corinthians 12.2–4)

For fellow Jews at the time he was writing, the third heaven was the highest heaven. It was paradise itself. For a moment, apparently, Paul felt himself to be transported out of this world and to be experiencing something of the very treasure of paradise. Now 14 years later, he recalls this precious moment. Using poetic repetition and language of negation ('things that are not to be told'), he points to some extraordinary, deep, mystical vision.

Thomas Aquinas also reported that he had some such mystical vision. Four months before his death, he had such a profound experience while saying mass that he stated, 'All I have written seems to me like so much straw compared with what I have seen and with what was revealed to me'. As a result, he simply abandoned his greatest theological work on which he had already been working for years.

I am always grateful when students discover this fact about Aquinas after studying his (sometimes difficult) theological writings rather than before doing so! What can easily be seen as an excuse for unscrewing our brains when going into church or studying the Christian faith, is really a reminder that faith, properly understood, finally goes beyond words.

In this lyrical passage Paul also points to some profound experience that in reality was quite beyond words. It had happened long ago and possibly it was never repeated. Yet it had continued to fuel his sense of grace ever since.

Almost immediately Paul moves away from the heights of this experience and back to human frailty. He is all too conscious that, by recalling such an experience, he might be seen to be boasting. There is a very real danger for Christians of spiritual pride. Just when we feel we have achieved something to be proud of, we realize that our very pride has already spoilt it:

> Therefore, to keep me from being too elated, a thorn was given me in the flesh, a messenger of Satan to torment me, to keep me from being too elated. Three times I appealed to the Lord about this, that it would leave me, but he said to me, 'My grace is sufficient for you, for power is made perfect in weakness.' So, I will boast all the more gladly of my weaknesses, so that the power of Christ may dwell in me. (2 Corinthians 12.7–9)

Again, scholars have long debated what this 'thorn in the flesh' actually was. Some have speculated it was a disability such as epilepsy, stammering, blindness or even manic-depression. Others have considered it to be a disease such as malaria and, others again, some enemy (which, of course, is the way the term 'thorn in the flesh' is now popularly used). Obviously we shall never know.

However, what is clear is that Paul made a direct connection between this mystical experience and his own frailty – his own thorn in the flesh. The two were both a part of the path leading to a sense of grace.

Once aware of this, he could see the suffering and persecution he had experienced in a fresh light: 'Therefore I am content with weaknesses, insults, hardships, persecutions, and calamities for the sake of Christ; for whenever I am weak, then I am strong' (2 Corinthians 12.10).

This, if you like, is the paradox of grace. As John Newton was later to discover, too, the very weaknesses of the human life can point us to grace. Only when we finally recognize our weaknesses, can we even see the need for grace. Then, through grace, can we be strong.

Sufficient grace.

MEDITATION
2 Corinthians 12.1–10

30

Grace and the moral gap

Perhaps this should be the most important difference between those of us who worship and those who don't. From our worship we should know that, if we are finally to be 'good', we need grace. Whereas other people might imagine they can be good on their own, worshippers should know that they need God's help to be good.

Of course, for most of the time people are 'good' out of caution, habit or upbringing. For example, when I walk around a supermarket, I am not seriously tempted to steal things. As a child I was taught quite clearly that such stealing was wrong, so not stealing has now become little more than a habit. I do not even need the threat of being arrested and imprisoned to persuade me not to steal. Frankly, it simply never even occurs to me to steal. Nor do my friends praise me for being morally good for not stealing.

However, change the situation somewhat and see what happens. Supposing I had been brought up to steal, or that I am desperately hungry but am without any money. Now I might be strongly tempted to steal from the same supermarket. In these new circumstances, not stealing might require an enormous act of will on my part. In addition, other people might now admire me for not stealing.

Moral goodness is most evident in situations of serious temptation. The greater the temptation, the more difficult it is to be good, and the more apparent goodness is when it occurs. Three of the Gospels give accounts of serious temptation at the very start of Jesus' ministry. For Jesus the temptations, during his 40 days of fasting in the wilderness, were about misusing God-given powers for selfish human ends. Perhaps, the tempter suggests, Jesus could perform some miracle to satisfy his physical hunger, to impress the masses, or to gain wealth and political power. The temptations were strong and real. Yet, through grace, he overcame them: 'Worship the Lord your God, and serve only him' (Matthew 4.10).

The term 'the moral gap' has been coined to explain what is going on here. In Christian belief there is no moral gap in the life of Jesus (a theme that will be explored next week). However, there is an obvious moral gap ever-present in the lives of the rest of us.

Let me explain. Worshippers, especially, should have a strong sense of moral duty. Within worship, after all, Christians are commanded to 'love your enemies and pray for those who persecute you' (Matthew 5.41). We are even told, 'Be perfect, therefore, as your heavenly Father is perfect' (Matthew 5.48). Yet we are also reminded, every time we go to church, that we are anything but perfect. In almost every church service we are invited to confess our sins and to acknowledge our wretchedness.

The moral gap is the yawning chasm between our strong moral duty and our own obvious sinfulness.

And it is in situations of serious temptation that this moral gap becomes most obvious. In these situations, we know all too well what our duty is, but self-interest persuades us to do otherwise:

- We know we should tell the truth, but all too often we protect ourselves by not doing so.
- We know we should be loving and caring to others, but at times it is just too tempting not to be.
- We know we should be generous to strangers in need, but we justify spending money unnecessarily on ourselves instead.
- We know we live in an increasingly fragile world, but we continue to exploit it.
- We know we should be peacemakers, but we still allow wars to happen.

- We know we should act to address some wrong, but we just watch.
- We know we should be humble and patient, but we are still arrogant and self-righteous.
- We know we should worship God with all our heart and mind and soul, but we more readily think about ourselves . . .

Somewhere in this list you will see yourself. That is the moral gap.

Once this gap is identified, the need for grace becomes clear. If we cannot bridge the moral gap on our own, then we are seriously in need of the grace of God to do so. The grace of God can inspire us to act against our selfish desires, can shape us as we do so, and can sustain us afterwards. If only we allow grace to do so . . .

In the final chapter of his letter to the Corinthians, Paul writes:

> Examine yourselves to see whether you are living in the faith. Test yourselves. Do you not realize that Jesus Christ is in you? – unless, indeed, you fail to meet the test! I hope that you find out that we have not failed. (2 Corinthians 13.5–6)

And at the very end of the letter, Paul concludes fittingly: 'The grace of the Lord Jesus Christ, the love of God, and the communion of the Holy Spirit be with you all' (2 Corinthians 13.13).

MEDITATION
2 Corinthians 13.1–13

WEEK 6

Full of Grace

―――・>・＋・<・―――

31

Grace and favour

Week 6 returns to the Gospels to understand grace. It also explores grace through a series of sacred images.

The Greek word for 'grace' occurs frequently in Paul's letters but only occasionally in the Gospels. Even within them, the word is used only in Luke and John. The first three meditations in Week 6 will be taken from Luke and the final three from John. Together they offer a new dimension to a sense of grace. They allow us to move beyond grace in our own lives and to see grace, in all its fullness, as an expression of the uniqueness of Jesus' life. Through grace we are offered a glimpse of the most important Christian mystery – a glimpse of what it means to say that Jesus Christ is God.

The opening chapter of Luke's Gospel offers the first clue. In the story an angel greets the young Mary at Nazareth:

'Greetings, favoured one! The Lord is with you.' But she was much perplexed by his words and pondered what sort of greeting this might be. The angel said to her, 'Do not be afraid, Mary, for you have found favour with God. And now, you will conceive in your womb and bear a son, and you will name him Jesus. He will be great, and will be called the Son of the Most High. (Luke 1.28–32)

In Greek the work translated 'favour' here (and, similarly, the word 'favourable') is also the word for 'grace'. Most translations (going back to the King James Bible) use the word 'favour'. The New English Bible, however, translates it as: 'Do not be afraid, Mary, for God has been gracious to you.' 'Grace' and 'favour' being used to mean much the same thing – as they do in the phrase 'a grace and favour residence' (traditionally, a residence belonging to the Crown lent to a distinguished person as free accommodation).

Whichever translation is used, the meaning is the same. God is showing especial favour or grace to Mary by allowing her to bring the Son of God into the world. Of course she is perplexed and terrified. However, she is reassured by the angel in Luke's story: 'The Holy Spirit will come upon you, and the power of the Most High will overshadow you; therefore the child to be born will be holy; he will be called Son of God' (Luke 1.35).

There is a long custom in the eastern church of showing especial reverence to Mary as 'God-bearer'. She alone was shown God's especial grace and favour.

I will never forget a visit to see the Black Madonna of Czestochowa in Poland. I had been invited to take part in an international conference of Franciscans at Warsaw. Whatever their nationality they tended to use Italian as their common language. They laughed, joked and teased each other in Italian, but (thank goodness) gave most of their papers in English. They even gesticulated to each like real Italians. And their hospitality and friendliness to an Anglican visitor was splendidly Italian.

On the Sunday after mass in their chapel at Warsaw, it was planned that as a treat we should go by coach to Czestochowa to see the Black Madonna. We were soon on our way down the motorway. As the coach approached the church at

Czestochowa we could see crowds of people everywhere. The Franciscans, still laughing and joking, hurried off to find their special contact. Soon they returned and beckoned me to follow. We were taken through a small door and found ourselves being ushered along a series of dark corridors away from the crowds outside. 'Come this way!' they kept saying to me, waving their arms about as they did so.

Suddenly we were in the great church itself. In fact we were right in the choir in the middle of high mass. Behind us was a packed congregation and next to us was a wedding couple. The priest was actually giving communion to the couple as we barged into the church. Most curiously of all, nobody paid any attention to us whatsoever. For them it seemed to be perfectly natural to see a group of friars entering the choir through a secret door, gazing at the Black Madonna behind the high altar, and then leaving again back through the same secret door. My English sense of decorum was distinctly tickled.

Yet there was the celebrated Black Madonna. Only the mournful face of Mary and the infant Jesus could be seen – the faded varnish leaving the impression that their faces were black. Their bodies were covered by silver. This 'icon' has long been venerated by the Polish people and especially by Pope John Paul II, once the bishop of nearby Krakow. It has served as a symbol of a country that has suffered so much at the hands of different occupying powers, yet survived. And it continues to remind Polish Catholics of the special place of Mary in the story of God's grace.

Then Mary said, 'Here am I, the servant of the Lord; let it be with me according to your word.' (Luke 1.38)

MEDITATION
Luke 1.26–38

32

The link of grace

It is Luke who gives us stories of the childhood of Jesus. Matthew writes about the birth and escape to Egypt, but then jumps straight to adulthood. Mark and John offer nothing at all about birth or childhood. Luke alone has the stories of the presentation of the child Jesus in the temple, of Simeon and Anna, of Jesus growing up at Nazareth and of the 12-year-old Jesus listening to the teachers in the temple and asking them questions.

Luke also offers an important link with grace. Having written about the grace and favour showed to the young Mary, he now points to the same grace and favour in the child Jesus:

> When they had finished everything required by the law of the Lord, they returned to Galilee, to their own town of Nazareth. The child grew and became strong, filled with wisdom; and the favour of God was upon him. (Luke 2.39–40)

Again the word 'favour' here translates the Greek word for 'grace'. This time it is the King James Bible that brings this out: 'And the child grew, and waxed strong, filled with wisdom: and the grace of God was upon him.'

Luke also concludes the story of the boy Jesus asking questions in the temple in a similar way, using the word 'favour' or 'grace' once more:

> Then he went down with them and came to Nazareth, and was obedient to them. His mother treasured all these things in her heart. And Jesus increased in wisdom and in years, and in divine and human favour. (Luke 2.51–52)

Skilfully Luke suggests a crucial link. The grace of God that Christians know partially in their lives, can be seen in a special way first in Mary and then in the young Jesus.

Thirty years ago, when I first became the priest of a remote Northumberland parish, I was shown around the old school room at Ford by Meg Thompson. Then in her eighties, she still had strong memories of life at the turn of the nineteenth century. She remembered the smiling face and rotund figure of the priest at the time. And she recalled lessons, sitting at an ink-stained desk and surrounded by murals depicting scenes from the Bible. Every day, with unflagging enthusiasm and an almost impenetrable Northumbrian accent, she told one party of tourists after another the story of how these murals were created.

They were painted over two decades on detachable frames by the Victorian patroness of the parish, Lady Waterford. A rich and well-connected widow with strong evangelical convictions, she was determined to build a model Christian community here in rural Northumberland. Living in the castle at Ford, she relocated the entire village and rebuilt it in considerable style. Disapproving of alcohol, she closed the pub and opened a rather less popular milk bar instead. Villagers who still insisted upon drinking had a two-mile walk up hill to the pub in the next parish. When the old traditionalist, who had been rector of Ford for 50 years, finally died, she appointed a priest who shared her own convictions. In his affectionate autobiography he recalled that she had been particularly anxious to make sure, before appointing him to this rich living, that he did believe in the eternal punishments of hell. Apparently she considered this belief important for maintaining moral order. In turn, it was this priest that Meg Thompson still remembered from her childhood.

To teach the children of Ford about the Christian faith, Lady Waterford painted the extraordinary murals of biblical scenes in the newly built school. In order to make these scenes living and relevant, she used the villagers themselves as models for figures in the murals. Meg Thompson told visitors about each of these villagers, now long dead, but still very much alive in her memory.

I doubt if those trained in fine art would rank the murals highly. They are certainly much more skilful than I could ever manage myself – but that is not saying much. Lady Waterford asked the art critic John Ruskin what he thought of them at the time (he enjoyed patronizing the nobility), but even he gave a very evasive response.

Yet as images, in this setting, some are very striking indeed – especially the picture of the boy Jesus. Set in a panel on his own, he looks down from the wall on generations of children and now tourists. Of course he, too, has long blond hair and blue eyes. Meg could remember the man who had been the model as a child. His nephew, now 90 himself, was still living in the village. He had worked as the local rat catcher all his life. Sitting by a small coal fire, he left the front door open even in the middle of winter, long hardened to the cold. And he talked with pride about his uncle being chosen as the model by Lady Waterford all those years ago.

For these old villagers this was, uniquely, *their* boy Jesus. Grace shining through an amateur painting – linking them to grace in Jesus.

MEDITATION
Luke 2.39–52

33

Words of grace

The link of grace continues in Luke. He opens his account of Jesus' ministry with the powerful story of the rejection of Jesus at Nazareth. Mark, the earliest Gospel, gives a shorter version of this story but places it later. Luke places it in pole position and makes an explicit link to grace within it.

In Luke's story Jesus goes to the synagogue in his home town of Nazareth 'as was his custom'. By this stage in Jewish history the synagogue had already become important as a place of learning and teaching. Once the temple had been destroyed by the Romans in AD 70, the synagogue became and has remained the centre of Jewish worship. For the moment, at least, synagogue teaching (often led by laypeople) and temple ritual and worship existed side by side. Both, the Gospels suggest, were important to Jesus.

Jesus stands up, is given the scroll of Isaiah, unrolls it and reads the dramatic passage:

> The Spirit of the Lord is upon me,
> because he has anointed me
> to bring good news to the poor.
> He has sent me to proclaim release to the captives
> and recovery of sight to the blind
> to let the oppressed go free,
> to proclaim the year of the Lord's favour. (Luke 4.18–19)

He rolls the scroll up again, gives it back and sits down to teach:

> The eyes of all in the synagogue were fixed on him. Then he began to say to them, 'Today this scripture has been fulfilled

in your hearing.' All spoke well of him and were amazed at the gracious words that came from his mouth. (Luke 4.20–22)

Perhaps the translation 'gracious words' misses some of the meaning here. It is possible that Luke intends us simply to understand that Jesus spoke well (as in 'That was a gracious vote of thanks'). Yet, once again, the King James Bible suggests something much more than this: 'And all bare him witness, and wondered at the words of grace which proceeded out of his mouth.' Translating this phrase as 'words of grace' does make an important link back to the grace in the young Jesus already noted by Luke.

Within many churches faced with political oppression around the world, this story from Luke has become a key text. Here is Jesus teaching that his ministry is to fulfil Isaiah's prophecy 'to bring good news to the poor' and 'to let the oppressed go free'. These have proved to be potent words for those suffering from oppression and injustice.

I discovered a powerful symbol of this when visiting Cape Town soon after the release of Nelson Mandela from prison and the collapse of apartheid. We had the astonishing privilege of staying with that saint of the Anglican church, Archbishop Desmond Tutu. He had come as an older student to King's College, London, when I was still a very green undergraduate. Who could ever forget his dynamic (and tiny) figure rushing about King's, beaming openness and excitement? Once made bishop and then archbishop in South Africa, we had anxiously watched him on television, praying and hoping that he would not be murdered by one of those South Africans who deeply hated him. We had been in awe at his courage, both in opposing apartheid and in quelling violence among those themselves opposed to apartheid. Now, at this great moment of liberation, we had been invited to stay with him for a few days in the new South Africa.

Desmond Tutu took us with great pride to St George's, the

imposing Anglican cathedral in Cape Town. And there he showed us a beautiful little statue entitled African Madonna. Carved by Leon Underwood, it depicts Mary as a powerful African woman, resting the child Jesus on her broad left hip. She clasps Jesus with her two strong, working hands and gazes ahead with a face full of determination and purpose. The entire statue is ebony black, except that on her head she wears a golden crown. Here, indeed, in this statue is 'good news to the poor ... release to the captives'; here 'the oppressed go free'; and now, it seemed at this very moment in South Africa (however fleetingly), was the time 'to proclaim the year of the Lord's favour'.

In Luke's story it was, also, a fleeting moment. The crowd suddenly becomes sceptical:

> They said, 'Is not this Joseph's son?' He said to them, 'Doubtless you will quote to me this proverb, "Doctor, cure yourself!" ... Truly I tell you, no prophet is accepted in the prophet's home town'. (Luke 4.22–24)

Soon the crowd becomes murderous:

> When they heard this, all in the synagogue were filled with rage. They got up, drove him out of the town, and led him to the brow of the hill on which their town was built, so that they might hurl him off the cliff. But he passed through the midst of them and went on his way. (Luke 4.28–30)

The words of grace had not really been heard at all.

MEDITATION
Luke 4.14-30

34

Full of grace

The word 'grace' is used just four times in John's Gospel. All four are in the prologue in the opening chapter (John 1.1–18). Taken together they complete the links made in Luke.

Luke, as we have seen, points to a link between the special grace shown to the young Mary and the grace to be found in the child Jesus. Then, for a brief moment at the beginning of Jesus' adult ministry, people in his home town synagogue glimpse this grace for themselves. Yet, their mood changes almost immediately and any sense of grace evaporates as they try to murder him.

So, an important, but still elusive, link is suggested – between the fragile sense of grace known to ordinary people (the sense of God's help in their lives) and the grace uniquely at work first in Mary and then in Jesus. It is exactly this link that John's prologue helps us to understand better.

> In the beginning was the Word, and the Word was with God, and the Word was God. He was in the beginning with God. All things came into being through him, and without him not one thing came into being. What has come into being in him was life, and the life was the light of all people. The light shines in the darkness, and the darkness did not overcome it. (John 1.1–5)

This great prologue – read in countless Christmas midnight communion services – takes us right back to the beginning of the Bible: 'In the beginning when God created the heavens and the earth . . .' (Genesis 1.1). It was God's Word that created everything: 'Then God said, "Let there be light"; and there was light' (Genesis 1.3). This Word was 'the light of all people'.

And the Word became flesh and lived among us, and we
have seen his glory, the glory as of a father's only son, full
of grace and truth. (John testified to him and cried out, 'This
was he of whom I said, "He who comes after me ranks
ahead of me because he was before me"'). (John 1.14–15)

The Word that became flesh was not John the Baptist but Jesus
Christ. In the prologue it is Jesus Christ alone who is the
'father's only son, full of grace and truth'. This is what makes
Jesus Christ unique. Other people might have a fragile sense of
grace, but Jesus uniquely is 'full of grace'.

This combination of 'glory', 'grace' and 'truth' soon suggests another comparison in the prologue – this time between
Moses and Jesus:

The law indeed was given through Moses; grace and truth
came through Jesus Christ. No one has ever seen God. It is
God the only Son, who is close to the Father's heart, who
has made him known. (John 1.17–18)

The language echoes the account of the great patriarch Moses
receiving the ten commandments from God on Mount Sinai.
One of the most holy moments in the Jewish Bible. Moses
takes two tablets up the mountain early in the morning and
discovers that he is in the very presence of the Lord God:

The LORD descended in the cloud and stood with him there,
and proclaimed the name, 'The LORD.' The LORD passed
before him, and proclaimed,

'The LORD, the LORD,
a God merciful and gracious,
slow to anger,
and abounding in steadfast love . . . for the thousandth
    generation'
(Exodus 34.5–7)

In this Exodus story, it is God not Moses who is depicted as 'merciful and gracious'. John's prologue follows the same tradition: Moses merely receives the law. Jesus Christ, however, does share the divine attributes with the Father: grace and truth come through him. And that is why he uniquely makes God known to us.

A little more might be said at this point. Language used to depict God makes more sense if we can connect it (however faintly) with our own experience. For example, the term 'steadfast love' applied to God will probably make most sense to people who have already known human love. Just imagine someone who has never been loved by anyone. How would such a person make any sense of 'steadfast love'?

Of course this is not to confuse human and divine love. For a Christian they are obviously distinct. God's love is unfailing and steadfast, whereas human love is all too fickle. Yet, if no connection whatsoever is made between human and divine love, it is difficult to see how we can make any sense at all of divine love.

Perhaps, then, a tenuous connection might be made between the phrase 'full of grace' and our own sense of grace. As seen earlier, we can discover a sense of grace when we become aware of our own frailty. At such a moment we can have a (fleeting) sense that God is working in and through us. Now for a thought experiment. Try to imagine for a moment, someone who is not frail at all . . . someone who has a continuous sense of God working in and through him . . . someone so full of grace as to be without sin . . . someone who is grace personified. In other words, someone who is Jesus Christ . . .

Grace made flesh.

————•◆•————

MEDITATION
John 1.1–15

35

Grace upon grace

Grace made flesh . . .

A friend recently gave me a haunting image he has created. Recently retired from a distinguished career in academic medicine, he now takes an active role in medical ethics (which is how we first met) and in his local Anglican church. He is also a keen and imaginative photographer.

The image he gave me is a studio photograph entitled 'The Easter Story'. It shows two silver chalices and a paten set on a pale blue tablecloth, itself fading gently into a slightly paler but featureless background. The chalice on the left has a crown of thorns dangling from its rim, while the paten on the right has a crust, torn from a loaf, placed upon it. The chalice in the middle has been knocked over and the wine from it is seeping into the tablecloth.

This simple but striking image makes the crucial link between Jesus Christ – full of grace – and ourselves. The suffering and humiliation of Christ is represented in each of the silver vessels – the mock crown of thorns hanging on one, the spilt blood oozing from another, and the broken body resting on the third. Yet each vessel also mirrors ourselves. The silver of the three vessels reflects the church windows behind the camera and the busy world beyond. And the vessels are the ones that are used for communion on a Sunday in my friend's local church. This is the bread and wine for us to share together at Easter.

A link is subtly made in this image between the Easter story in the Gospels and Easter Eucharist today. Such a link is also made in John's prologue. You may already have spotted that one mention of 'grace' within it has so far gone unnoticed:

A Sense of Grace

'From his fullness we have all received, grace upon grace' (John 1.16).

Here is the link we have been looking for. Jesus Christ – not John the Baptist or even Moses – is the one who uniquely is 'full of grace', and it is from this fullness that we, in turn, can receive 'grace upon grace'. What we sense only dimly, we can find in abundance in Jesus Christ. In him we, too, can know grace more fully. If only we can respond, especially as we share the Eucharist together, we too can receive 'grace upon grace'.

John's Gospel uses a wealth of images to make this point again and again. Addressing the Samaritan woman at the well, Jesus uses the image of water:

'Everyone who drinks of this water will be thirsty again, but those who drink of the water that I will give them will never be thirsty. The water that I will give will become in them a spring of water gushing up to eternal life.' (John 4.13–14)

After the feeding of the 5,000, Jesus in John's Gospel adds the image of bread as well to make the same point: 'Jesus said to them, "I am the bread of life. Whoever comes to me will never be hungry, and whoever believes in me will never be thirsty"' (John 6.35).

It is John's Gospel that gives us the image of Jesus as the good shepherd (and even Jesus as the gate of the sheepfold). An image that has inspired paintings galore. And it is again John's Gospel that has the image of Jesus as the vine and we as the branches:

'I am the true vine, and my Father is the vinegrower. He removes every branch in me that bears no fruit . . . I am the vine, you are the branches. Those who abide in me and I in them bear much fruit, because apart from me you can do nothing.' (John 15.1–2 and 5)

Full of Grace

This great image is followed immediately in John's Gospel by Jesus' commandment to love:

> 'This is my commandment, that you love one another as I have loved you. No one has greater love than this, to lay down one's life for one's friends. You are my friends if you do what I command you. I do not call you servants any longer, because the servant does not know what the master is doing; but I have called you friends, because I have made known to you everything that I have heard from my Father. You did not choose me but I chose you.' (John 15.12–16)

That final sentence expresses exactly a Christian sense of grace. It is the sense that it is finally not our own doing, but rather God in Christ working in and through us. It is not us choosing to follow God or to be good, but rather God in Christ first calling us to worship and goodness.

Grace upon grace . . . if only we can respond.

MEDITATION
John 1.16–18

113

36

Grace on the cross

On my desk at home is a cross of nails. It reminds me of the day I was ordained in Coventry Cathedral – and, more importantly, of why I was ordained.

A cross of nails is made from the flat irons nails pulled from the wreckage of the old cathedral at Coventry. When I was a curate at nearby Rugby, many local people could still remember the terrible night in 1940 when German bombers flattened the city and all but destroyed the cathedral at its centre. After becoming Bishop of Coventry in 1956, Cuthbert Bardsley poured his energy into building a new cathedral alongside the old ruins. Using his great charm and enthusiasm, he managed to attract leading artists to contribute their skills to adorn this new cathedral – Piper to design the magnificent windows linking the old and new buildings, Epstein the haunting statue outside, and Sutherland the commanding but controversial tapestry of Christ in the chancel. When the new cathedral was consecrated six years later, excited crowds came to see it.

Cuthbert Bardsley was a man of warmth and vision. In his 20 years as Bishop of Coventry, he, and the many talented people he picked to work alongside him, pioneered many changes now accepted by others. And he was determined that this new cathedral, the product of war, should instead become a focus of reconciliation. The cross of nails was designed as the image of this reconciliation. Each cross of nails was made of three nails; two overlapping horizontal nails welded onto a larger vertical nail.

He was a dramatic preacher – it was rumoured that he had considered being an actor when young (as curates we affectionately referred to him as 'the acting bishop'). In his sermons

he often used the image of the cross of nails. The two horizontal nails might sometimes represent the twinned industrial
cities of Coventry and Dresden. However the vertical nail was
always to remind people – English and Germans alike – of
God our creator.

In his depiction of the final moments of Jesus on the cross,
Mark (and Matthew similarly) focuses upon the words of
apparent dereliction from the opening of the twenty-second
psalm:

> When it was noon, darkness came over the whole land until
> three in the afternoon. At three o'clock Jesus cried out with
> a loud voice, 'Eloi, Eloi, lema sabachthani?' which means,
> 'My God, my God, why have you forsaken me?' (Mark
> 15.33–34)

Luke is just as dramatic, but his focus is upon words of trust
and self-committal to God from the thirty-first psalm:

> It was now about noon, and darkness came over the whole
> land until three in the afternoon, while the sun's light failed;
> and the curtain of the temple was torn in two. Then Jesus,
> crying with a loud voice, said, 'Father, into your hands I
> commend my spirit.' (Luke 23.44–46)

John's Gospel is quite different. Here Jesus uniquely shows
concern about his mother and the disciple he loved, and then:

> After this, when Jesus knew that all was now finished, he
> said (in order to fulfil the scripture), 'I am thirsty.' A jar full
> of sour wine was standing there. So they put a sponge full
> of the wine on a branch of hyssop and held it to his mouth.
> When Jesus had received the wine, he said, 'It is finished.'
> Then he bowed his head and gave up his spirit. (John
> 19.28–30)

In the original Greek, 'It is finished', is stated in a single word. The New English Bible translates it as 'It is accomplished.' It could have been translated as 'It is completed' or even 'It is fulfilled.' There is a sense of purpose and direction in the Greek word that is missing from 'It is finished.'

This work of grace is now complete. Jesus has fulfilled the great commandment, to love: 'This is my commandment, that you love one another as I have loved you. No one has greater love than this, to lay down one's life for one's friends' (John 15.12–13).

After the terrible events of 11 September 2001 and its aftermath, Jesus' work of grace on the cross needs careful treatment. Too often in Christian history the idea of 'laying down one's life for one's friends' has been used to depict warriors risking their lives in battle. It is not too difficult to see how it might also be used to depict suicide bombers, especially those driven by religious conviction.

The cross is emphatically *not* about Jesus taking the lives of others. It is about Jesus giving his own life *for* others without taking other lives at all. In this final act of grace, Jesus fulfils the commandment to love others:

'And this is eternal life, that they may know you, the only true God, and Jesus Christ whom you have sent. I glorified you on earth by finishing the work that you gave me to do.' (John 17.3–4)

So, finally, grace on the cross.

———◆———

MEDITATION
John 19.25–30

Notes

1. All quotes in this section and Chapter 8 are taken from András Schiff, 'Playing Bach on the Piano', in *J. S. Bach Solo Keyboard Works,* Decca, 1996.

2. *Complete Mission Praise,* Marshall Pickering/Harper Collins, London, 1999.

3. John Newton, *The Life of John Newton,* London, 1855 [no publisher given], p. 2.

4. Newton, *The Life of John Newton,* p. 4.

5. Newton, *The Life of John Newton,* p. 40.

6. Newton, *The Life of John Newton,* pp. 39–40.

7. Newton, *The Life of John Newton,* p. 46.

8. Newton, *The Life of John Newton,* p. 40.

9. Newton, *The Life of John Newton,* p. 41.

10. Newton, *The Life of John Newton,* p. 46.

11. Newton, *The Life of John Newton,* pp. 180–81.

12. Newton, *The Life of John Newton,* p. 233.